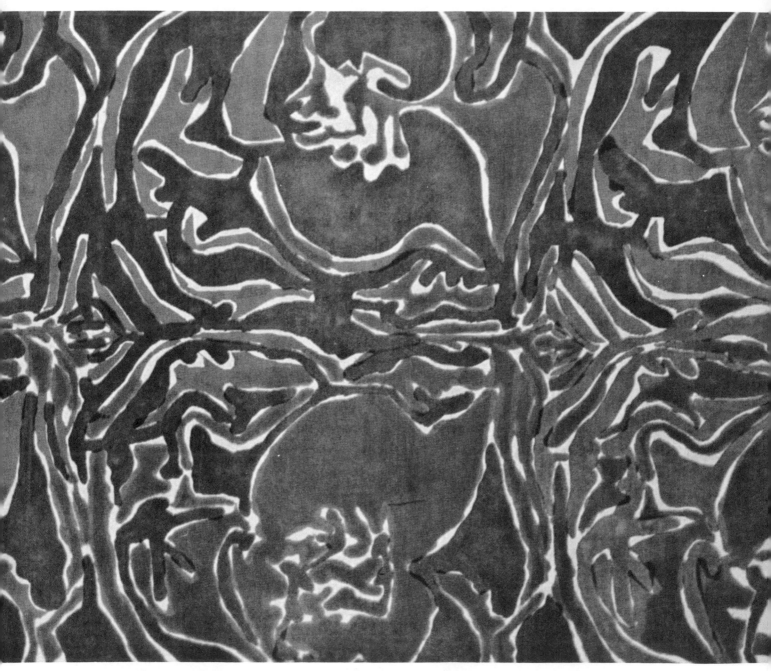

Fig. 1–5. (Reproduced in full color between pages 16 and 17.) The design for "Simple Grace" was screen-printed on fabric and then painted. (By Irene Naik)

SILK-SCREEN PRINTING
FOR ARTISTS & CRAFTSMEN

Mathilda V. Schwalbach & James A. Schwalbach

Dover Publications, Inc.
New York

We shamelessly dedicate this book to each other
because of our joys and stimulations in a common interest
that has made this all possible

This Dover edition, first published in 1980, is an unabridged and corrected version of the book originally published by Van Nostrand Reinhold Co., New York, in 1970, under the title *Screen Process Printing for Serigraphers and Textile Designers.*

International Standard Book Number: 0-486-24046-0
Library of Congress Catalog Card Number: 80-66838

Manufactured in the United States of America
Dover Publications, Inc.
31 East 2nd Street
Mineola, N.Y. 11501

CONTENTS

ACKNOWLEDGMENTS

For developing a climate and environment that made it possible for the creative artist-craftsman, both faculty and student, to develop freely and produce his work . . . . to the University of Wisconsin, Madison, and the Department of Related Art (Chairman, Professor Agatha Norton) in the School of Family Resources and Consumer Sciences.

For allocating time and facilities for the artist-teacher and his students to work and create, and particularly for the recognition of the production of the art object as the full scholarly equivalent of the more traditional academic research . . . . to the University of Wisconsin Center System (Chancellor Lorentz H. Adolfson), and especially to the University Center campuses at Baraboo and Janesville.

For the financing and building of the Allen-Related Art Textile Collection which stimulates both faculty and student in their quest for high quality production . . . . to the late Professor Helen Allen of the Department of Related Art.

For continuing encouragement and guidance . . . . to Professor Agnes Leindorff, Professor Ruth D. Davis, and Mrs. Patricia K. Mansfield.

For cooperation and assistance . . . . to Mrs. Ruth Harris, and Professor Margaret Cooper.

For gentle needling that kept one continually creating, sometimes under difficult arrangements . . . . to Professor Fred Logan of the Department of Art.

For the use of both themselves and their work within this book and for their complete cooperation in the many successes and failures we jointly experienced in our explorations . . . . to the following students: Carole Bansemer, Linda Baumgarten, Bobette Heller, Caroline Hunkel Kitelinger, Barbara C. Knollenberg, Jan Kraft, Patricia K. Mansfield, Margaret Mezzera, Timothy J. McIlrath, Irene Naik, Sue Palm, Russell Peterson, Sue C. Powell, James Prebonich, Karene Skarsten, Mrs. Elizabeth Weber, Robert Witzack, Patricia Zuzinec, and those many hundreds of other students from whom artist-teachers learn so much.

For the typing, proofing, and duplicating that never seemed to end . . . . to Mrs. Sharon L. Abraham, Mrs. Beatrice Goldberg, Miss Mary Hamel, and Miss Jan Norsetter.

For most sympathetic aid in the editing of this book . . . . to Mrs. Eleanore W. Karsten.

For initial interest in this project and his production of almost all of the photographs that appear in this book . . . . to Mr. Henry Kakehashi of the International Film Bureau in Chicago.

For permission to use copyright material. . . . to the American Center for Students and Artists, for the lines by Elizabeth McCausland from *Parnassus*, March 1940; the Print Council of America, for the definition from *What Is an Original Print*; and Yale University Press, for the quote from *Josef Albers: Despite Straight Lines*, by François Bucher.

INTRODUCTION

The realm of the artist-designer and individual printer is the major emphasis of this book, but we have made some effort to juxtapose it with the tremendously large and important screen-process industry that is such a lively part of the field of commercial graphic communication. Furthermore, we have endeavored to produce a book that would be useful to the amateur as well as the professional, to the very young artist and his teacher, and to the experienced producer. Screen-process printing is both simple and extremely complicated. This book discusses the process as it might be used in an elementary-school environment with students as young as eight or nine working with available and inexpensive materials. It also includes ideas that should interest the advanced textile designer and serigrapher.

This is a technical book. Technical books (or as they are sometimes called in a derogatory manner, how-to-do-it books) are always difficult to produce because of the overriding interest most beginners and many advanced artists have in new techniques. Many creative people lose their creativity in the vast wonderland of methodology. One would not wish (at least not for any amount of time) to listen to musical scales played by the New York Philharmonic under the direction of Leonard Bernstein. But just as painful would be the rendition of a Brahms concerto by a third-rate orchestra. So while this is a book about techniques and skills, the authors have attempted to continually remind the reader that skills are not the end goal—they are only a helpful preliminary. They are necessary to produce meaningful results but they are no guarantee of quality production. And the goal of all should be quality production.

Fig. 1–1. The walls of Gargas Cave in the French Pyrenees are covered with records of prehistoric man's culture. Shown here are negative prints of mutilated hands.

1. STENCILS—A SHORT HISTORY

In prehistoric times, when his castle was a mere hole in a hill, man left a visual record of his culture. On the walls of three caves—Gargas near Aventignan in the French Pyrenees, its small neighbor, Tibiran, and Maltravieso in the Spanish province of Estremadura—there are more than 200 prints of hands, most of them mutilated by sickness or accident. Their meaning can only be conjectured, but a close study clearly shows them to be a form of aesthetic expression. The idea of repetition, the feeling of rhythm that emerges from the images and the intervening space, and the horizontal alignment suggest a definite notion of artistic decoration.

These handprints are black (from the manganese deposits scraped from the walls of the cave) and red (obtained from ocher, a clayey earth colored with iron oxides). The positive prints were made by pressing a hand covered with color on the wall of the cave in the manner of a relief print. The negative prints (Fig. 1–1), which give the effect of a halo, were made by placing a hand on the wall and spraying the color over and around it. The color was blown directly from the mouth or, more likely, through a short piece of hollow bone. Thus spray painting, stencil printing, and relief printing were invented sometime around thirty thousand years before the birth of Christ. Man literally left his imprint on the wall of his cave to express symbolically and aesthetically his eternal needs.

The earliest stencils do not survive because they were made of leaves and skins and deteriorated rapidly. Some experts claim that the first stencils used by prehistoric man were some found in the Fiji Islands that were made from leaves from bamboo trees. When the leaves fell they curled up, and worms or larvae ate holes in them. Unrolled, they served as stencils for the primitive islanders to decorate garments with vegetable dyes. Later on these same islanders used heated banana leaves for cutting their stencil patterns, which they printed on a thin bark stripped from the malo tree.

Quintilian, in Italy during the early Christian era, was said to have taught children the alphabet by having them trace the letters through stencils. And several rulers living in the sixth century A.D. used stencil methods to attach their signatures to important documents.

In the Far East the Chinese and Japanese between 500 and 1000 A.D. developed the art of stenciling to a high level. Buddhism was rising in importance, and the faithful were encouraged to seek favor of Buddha by duplicating his picture as frequently as possible. This was best accomplished with a stencil. In the famous Caves of the Thousand Buddhas at Tun Huang, in western China, which was a strategic trade center and gathering place for Chinese, Turks, and Tibetans, one finds religious caves dug into the sandstone and extending for a half mile along the hillside. The walls of these grottoes are covered with images of Buddha. He is usually seated and sometimes surrounded by his faithful attendants. Some of the Buddha images are only a few inches high, while others tower 70 feet up the cave wall. A few are carved, but many are stenciled. Some, which are still unfinished, reveal the characteristic light-gray lines made by the thousands of little holes pricked in the stencil to duplicate the pattern.

Fig. 1–2. Noh robe of the late eighteenth or early nineteenth century, gold stenciled on red colored silk. (Art Institute of Chicago, Gift of Robert Allerton)

Stenciled silks from China borrowed many symbols from the various religious faiths: Confucianism, Buddhism, and Taoism. The swastika, peacock, royal dragon, and conventionalized clouds and waves and various flowers shaded in the manner of embroidery also were stencil motifs. Since Chinese silks were much sought after in the Western world, it is probable that it was through them that the art of stenciling was introduced to Western cultures.

While not much is known about it, another method of producing a stencil was used in China in later years. An acid ink was used to draw or paint the design on stencil paper. The acid in the ink ate through the paper, leaving a clear-cut stencil.

In eighteenth-century Japan, which was closed to trade with the outside world, stencils were developed that might be described as the forerunners of today's screen-process stencil. The highly skilled Japanese stencil cutters were able to cut extremely intricate patterns, but they were limited by the necessity of bridging the floating parts of the stencil. (The center island in the letter "O" is an excellent example of a floating part.) They soon developed a method whereby a varnish, called *shibu*, was painted over a single cut-stencil sheet. The stencil paper was often handmade from the fibers of mulberry leaves. Since the people were very thrifty, they sometimes used discarded documents for stencils, and some valuable records have therefore been saved that otherwise would have been lost. Fine threads of silk or human hairs were used to tie in floating parts to the main section of the cut stencil (Fig. 1–3). The varnish held the hair in place. Often the hairs were stretched in a crisscross grid pattern about one quarter of an inch apart. In extremely complicated stencils the thin threads were tied by hand or with a special hook. After all the floating parts had been secured with thin threads, a second identical stencil was cut, varnished, then placed over the first stencil, with the two varnished sides facing each other. This was dried under pressure, producing an extremely strong

Fig. 1–3. In the Yuzen style of Japanese stencil production, developed in the eighteenth century, a grid of fine silk threads or hairs secures the floating parts of the stencil. (From the Helen Allen Textile Collection, Department of Related Arts, University of Wisconsin)

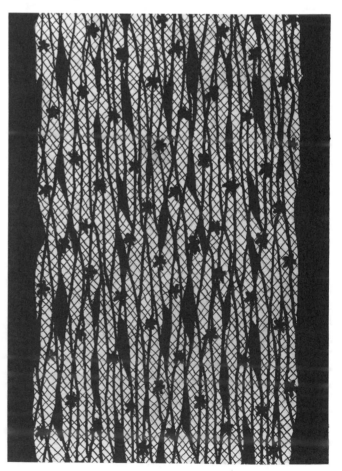

and durable stencil. The supporting threads were so thin that their effects could hardly be seen on prints from the stencils.

So now, for the first time, floating parts were held in place without the traditional bridges characteristic of earlier stencils. This process, called the Yuzen style by the Japanese, made possible new complexities in designing, but it was very tedious and difficult. Only the most skilled craftsmen could accomplish it. While it would seem to be only one easy step from this difficult grid system of fine threads or hairs to the use of an excellent grade of woven silk as the carrier for a stencil design, it was not until late in the nineteenth century, almost 150 years later, that this was done.

In Europe during the Middle Ages color was used on prints depicting various saints and on some playing cards. Wood blocks printed the basic design in black, and then the printer applied colors to these prints with very simple, crude stencils. Also, during this period, thousands of knights headed for the Holy Land and the Crusades needed red crosses on their clothing to identify them. The designers stretched a fine cloth made from hair over iron hoops from old wine casks. Pitch or ship's tar was used as a resist to block out the areas that would remain white, and the red cross was printed through the unfilled parts of the cloth on clothing and banners. In this manner the red cross could easily be duplicated many times over.

No one knows at what early date Nigerians formulated their stencil methods. They use stencils to print portions of fabric with a starch made from the cassava root. These starched areas resist the characteristic indigo dye while the unstarched areas accept it.

In 1868, Owen Jones published *Grammar of Ornament*, one of the most important works on decoration published in the nineteenth century. It illustrated various styles of ornament and contained many color plates. By 1910 the book had gone through nine editions and had been responsible for a considerable change in the types of stencil designs wallpaper and textile designers were producing. William Morris, the great nineteenth-century designer who was responsible for a revival in the field of decoration, was greatly influenced by Owen Jones and his work. Many of Morris's textile and wallpaper designs, though not directly copied from Jones, reflect his basic design philosophy, especially in the rich organic quality of decoration. The *Art Nouveau* of the late nineteenth century also owes some of its ideas to Owen Jones, particularly the strong feeling for growing things evident in *Art Nouveau* patterns.

Honors for the development of screen-process printing into a major craft must be given to the commercial printing industry and, in the United States, to the advertising and sign-painting industries. While there has been more activity in the United States in this century, it was in Germany and the Lyons district of France around 1870 that the pioneer work was accomplished. Here silk was used

Fig. 1-4. An early hand-cut Japanese stencil. (Art Institute of Chicago, Frederick W. Gookin collection)

as the stencil carrier. The first recorded patent for the use of silk was awarded to Samuel Simon of Manchester, England, in 1907. However, Mr. Simon printed his stencils with a stiff bristle brush charged with color instead of the rubber squeegee so common today.

In 1914, John Pilsworth, a commercial artist from San Francisco, perfected a multicolor screen process called the Selectasine method, for which he was later granted a patent in collaboration with a Mr. Owen. Only one screen was used. Like reduction color methods in relief and process printing, the largest color area, often the background, was printed first. Then, part of the design was blocked out with glue, and it was printed again with a second color over parts of color number one. Then a still smaller area was blocked out and printed with a third color. This went on until the final print was finished.

It was the lively competition between commercial sign painters and small print shops that sparked the early development of the screen-process craft in the United States. For a time each firm jealously guarded its own variations as house secrets. But by the time the Screen Process Printing Association, International, was founded in 1948, this commercial printing process was public property and a rapidly expanding industry.

In the textile industry even before World War I, stencils made of cardboard and zinc were used, and the color was applied with stiff brushes. This method, called brush painting, was soon replaced by the spraygun, but the same kind of stencils continued to be used. Then France became the first country to use screen-process printing for textiles in the early 1920s.

The screen process was used at the time by sign-painting firms in the United States, where its initial great expansion was due to the formation of grocery chains. They needed many inexpensive signs, which had to be produced by local sign painters because they were changed frequently. Sign shops that went into screen-process printing were able to underbid the traditional hand-brush sign painters. However, the image produced by these early screen-process sign printers was crude, particularly along the edges of the color areas. Because of this, the more polished letter-press and lithograph industry continued to make signs.

In 1925 the automatic screen-process printing machine was invented, which made it possible to print faster than the ink would dry. Unfortunately, the industry was not large enough at this time to induce paint manufacturers to produce fast-drying inks for screen printing. In 1929 a screen printer in Dayton, Ohio, Louis F. D'Autremont, developed a knife-cut stencil-film tissue that gave a print a clean, sharp edge. No longer was the crude, ragged edge a characteristic feature of the screen print. This new film

was patented by an associate of D'Autremont, A. S. Danemon, and sold under the commercial name of Profilm. The film was improved upon a few years later with the introduction of Nufilm, which was the invention of Joseph Ulano. It was easier to cut, adhered more easily to the silk, and therefore saved considerable time.

With the invention of Profilm and Nufilm the craft boomed. It was large enough now to be attractive to paint manufacturers, and many different kinds of paint were especially produced to be used in screen printing. With faster-drying inks, the automatic printing machines were further developed and took over most of the industry. Today these machines and the new inks can produce 2,000 to 3,000 impressions an hour.

During the early 1930s, the opening of Rockefeller Center in New York created a design sensation. It was the birth of another important style, which today's design historians refer to as Art Deco. It was a form of decoration that had its major roots in Cubism, American Indian crafts, and Egyptian design motifs. It found its first great expression in the decorative patterns in Radio City Music Hall, and it greatly affected the character of the textile and wallpaper designs produced by screen-process printers during the 1930s and 1940s.

Although the photographic process in screen printing has not been extensively used until recently, the original experimentation dates back to the late nineteenth century. Some of the principles were first developed in England by such men as Mongo Ponton and Sir Joseph W. Swan, working mostly in the printing of textiles and wallpaper. Since 1914, in the United States, there has been a similar active development of photographic screen-process printing with about twenty different photographic screen-process plates having been developed.

Why, with all this feverish and rapid development in the screen-process industry, was the fine artist so slow in picking up the medium as part of his expressive vocabulary? It was due partly to the secrecy prevalent in the commercial screen industry and partly to the natural suspicion and distaste that many artists have for anything so predominantly commercial as was the industry. This lack of interest must also be explained by the fact that artists before the 1930s showed little interest in *any* of the graphic-arts processes.

Credit for the development of screen-process printing as a fine-art medium belongs to two men, Anthony Velonis and Carl Zigrosser. During the 1930s the great De-

Fig. 1–5. Wallpaper printing at Jack Denst Designs Inc., Chicago.

pression sparked the formation of the WPA Federal Arts Project. A separate silk-screen unit of this project was set up in New York under the direction of Anthony Velonis. Early artists working in this area were Guy McCoy, Hyman Warsager, Edward Landon, Elizabeth Olds, Harry Gottlieb, Mervin Jules, Ruth Gikow, and Harry Sternberg. In 1938 the first one-man showing of silk-screen prints was held at the Contemporary Art Gallery in New York with the works of Guy McCoy. In the March 1940 issue of *Parnassus* magazine, Elizabeth McCausland reviewed McCoy's exhibition and wrote: "There is an exciting historical portent in the speed with which the silkscreen color print has captured the fancy of contemporary graphic artists."

But recognition for this new artistic medium was not automatic. Major credit for interesting the artist, the public, and particularly art collectors, museums, galleries, and art critics must go to Carl Zigrosser, eminent curator of prints of the Philadelphia Museum of Fine Arts. To distinguish the fine-art product from that produced by the screen-process industry, Zigrosser coined the term serigraph (*seri* means silk in Greek and *graph* means to draw). This term has since been generally accepted by screen-print artists. Albert Kosloff, at the end of World War II, attempted to give the screen-process print produced by the industry the term mitograph (from the Greek prefix *mitos* meaning threads or fibers and the suffix *graphein* meaning to write or draw). He reasoned that many other materials are used in contemporary screen-process printing as the carrier for the stencil besides silk—cotton, linen, nylon, organdy, copper, brass, bronze, and stainless-steel fibers. However, by then "silk-screen print" had been abandoned by the industry in favor of "screen-process print," which continues to designate the commercial product today.

Another major force in the development of serigraphy as a fine art was the formation in 1940 of the National Serigraph Society. It has set standards of excellence and has sent hundreds of exhibitions of its members' work to countries all over the world. These exhibitions are responsible for a good deal of museum interest in the purchase of original prints as part of museum collections.

Before the development of the massive automatic machines for the screen-process printing of textiles, commercial textile-printing firms printed their stencil repeats with an airbrush. Hard paper and even copper stencils were cut, laid on the fabrics, and the designs airbrushed. This method made delicate color gradations possible. However, it was a slow and costly method and has been replaced by speedier machine screening.

Recently, a form of stencil printing using painting brushes has reappeared. The process, known as *pochoir*, was used in France years ago for making stenciled reproductions of fine paintings, especially watercolors and *gouaches*. It is particularly useful, in the hands of a skilled technician, for the accurate reproduction of watercolors because the printing medium is a brush and fine

artist's grade watercolors. The color is simply painted through the cut stencil, and usually a screen frame is not used. A few artists have recently experimented with *pochoir* for the creative production of original prints.

Unlike the format of regular repeats established historically by wood-block printers, the large fashion prints that appeared in the 1960s were free and seemingly at random (Fig. 1–6). The repeats are so large and the prints so complex and irregular that one's eye is kept moving over the fabric. The problem of printing each repeat in exactly the right place is minimized. Other contemporary prints are often engineered precisely for the way the cloth will be cut in the manufacture of a specific garment, with no repeats at all. Any change in the printing would spoil the style and render the fabric useless for that particular garment. This coordination of the printed design and the finished piece of clothing is very helpful in the garment trade and is practiced in the fashion industry.

Helen Giambruni says in the May/June 1968 issue of *Crafts Horizon* magazine, in an article titled "Color Scale and Body Scale": "It should be remembered, however, that simplification of shape in clothing design preceded the print revival [of the 1960s] and, indeed, was probably one of its causes; shift-type dresses almost demand the use of prints for variety."

Another new technique, called Ambiente, for printing by use of machinery, has been developed by Timo and Pi Sarpaneva of Helsinki, Finland. Details of the method have not been made public, but the pattern is printed on both sides of the fabric. Any fabric can be used, and the patterns we have seen suggested free, brushed, expressionistic stripes or waves, either horizontal or vertical, that blended into each other in an almost unlimited range of colors.

The textile industry has found that screen prints have an advantage over the faster roller printing of textiles because screen colors penetrate the cloth much more deeply. This results in the brighter colors that became quite popular in the 1960s.

During the final years of our century we can expect such innovations in textile printing as paper-transfer printing, a heat-applied paper transfer with thermoplastic inks.

While the fine art of serigraphy has assured itself an important place in the history of art, it is probably too soon to evaluate its real consequence. This is also true of screen-process textile printing. However, one thing seems certain. The extreme versatility of the medium has opened completely new possibilities for design and expression to both the serigrapher and the textile designer, and the inexpensiveness of the equipment needed for small printing has also encouraged experimentation in design.

Fig. 1–6. Entitled "Paisley," this large random design is screen-printed on dotted swiss. (By Sue Palm)

Fig. 2–1. This youngster produced the design he is printing by painting the resist directly onto the screen with fingernail lacquer.

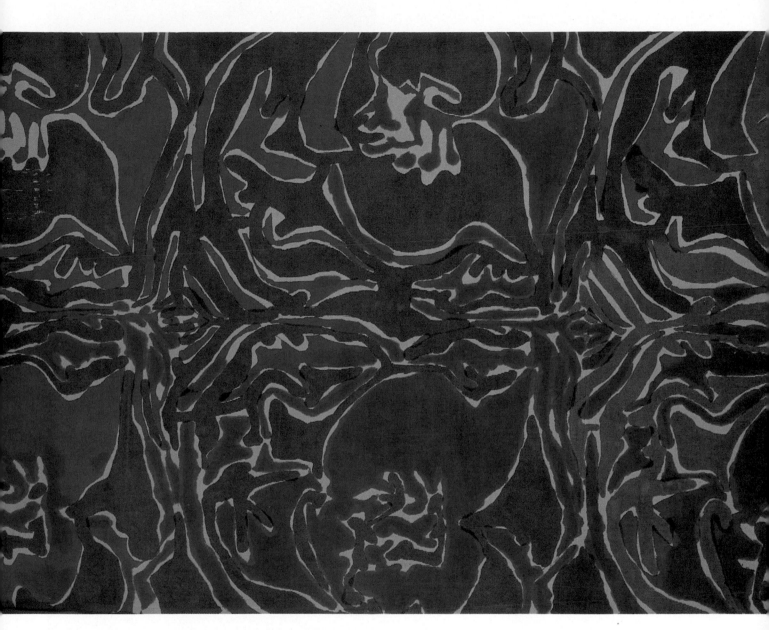

Fig. 1–5. (See Frontispiece.) The design for "Simple Grace" was screen-printed on fabric and then painted. (By Irene Naik)

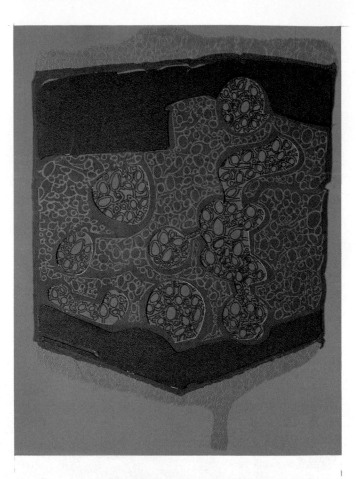

Fig. 2–7. (See pages 19 and 20.) The design for this serigraph, entitled "David's Shield," was drawn on transparent acetate and exposed on a light-sensitive emulsion resist. (By James A. Schwalbach)

Fig. 2–8. (See pages 19 and 20.) The fiber-reactive dye pastes used in this fabric print are easy to prepare. The designer has painted free, expressive lines after screen-printing the basic design, and where the two merge new colors are created. ("Purpled Scarf," by Irene Naik)

(See pages 32 and 33.) The final steps in a print for the beginner.

Fig. 4–41. (See pages 52 and 53.) This progression shows what the serigraph looks like after each of the five colors has been added.

Fig. 5–13. (See pages 64 and 65.) Two strikingly different effects are achieved in basically the same way. Seed pods, dried stalks of grain, and cut paper were used to make the designs on light-sensitive resists, and overlapping in the printing process built up the pattern sequences. (Top, by Barbara C. Knollenberg; bottom, by Patricia Zuzinec)

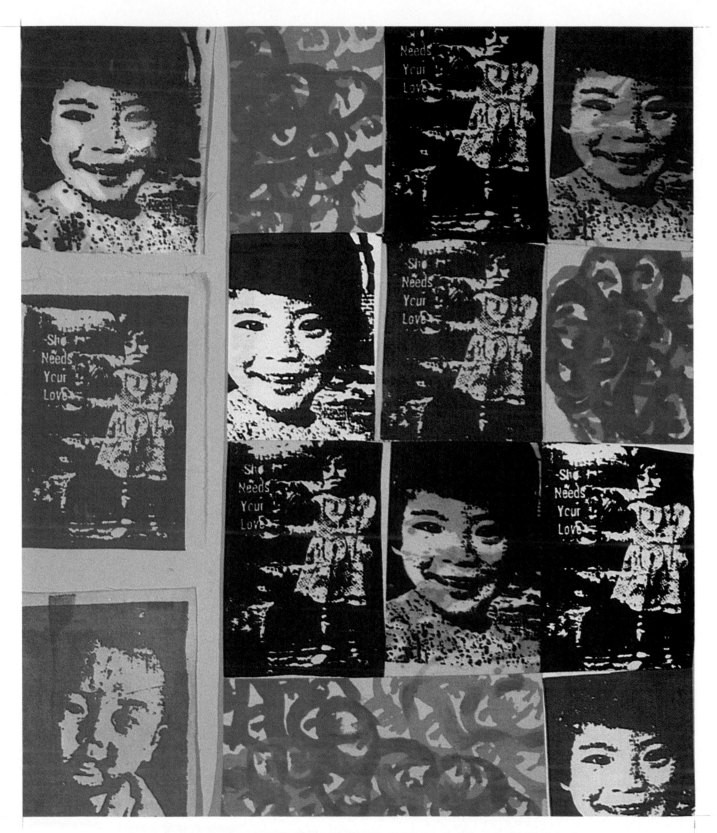

Fig. 6–12. (See pages 88 and 89.) Textile pattern composed of images in a light-sensitive film stencil made with a dry-copier transparency from current press cuttings produces a social commentary banner. (By Bobette Heller)

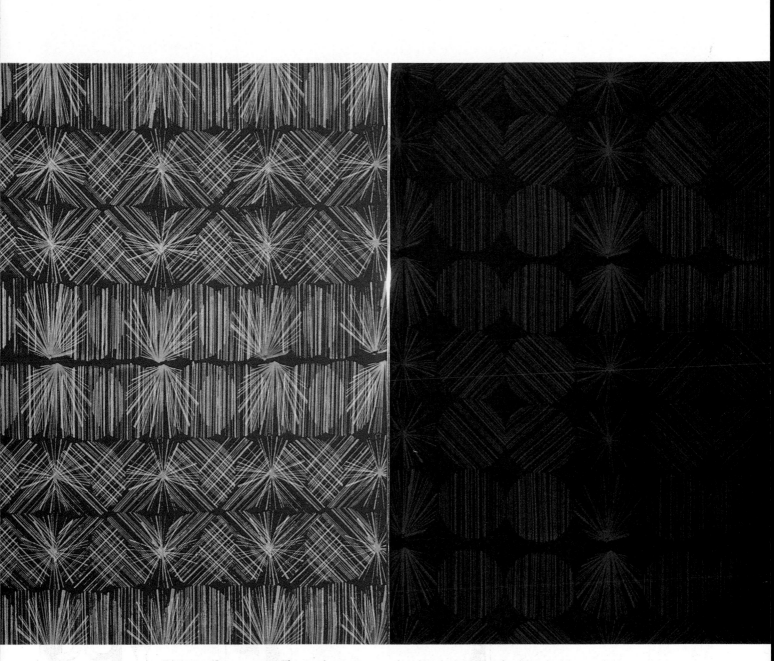

Fig. 7–14. (See page 105.) This textile print was produced by discharging color from the fabric with a stencil. ("Morning Snow," by Timothy J. McIlrath)

Fig. 8–5. (See pages 124 and 125.) Light-sensitive emulsion resists were used to make two very different designs, one a textile print entitled "November Feathers" and the other a serigraph called "Signs of the Times." (Textile, top, by Mathilda V. Schwalbach; serigraph, bottom, by James A. Schwalbach)

2. WHAT IS SCREEN PRINTING?

When Johnny places his jam-covered hand on the door of the refrigerator, Johnny is printing. And it is a form of printing that is the major concern of this book. Modern screen-process printing is merely a much more sophisticated method. It really is a contemporary but distant relative of both the ancient handprints on the walls of Gargas Cave and Johnny's jam print.

Four Different Types of Printing

Printing can be divided into four basic types: relief, intaglio, planographic, and stencil.

Relief and stencil printing are the oldest forms of printing. Along with those stenciled handprints on the walls of Gargas Cave, you will remember, there were handprints made by covering the surface of the hand with paint and then pressing it on the wall. *The images in relief printing stands out on the surface of the printing block.* This raised surface (Fig. 2–2) is then coated with ink and pressed on paper or fabric, and the image is printed. Newspapers, many magazines, linoleum block prints, and woodcuts are printed by means of relief printing. Fabrics are printed with linoleum or wood blocks and also with large roller presses that use wooden or copper rollers. This is a very common way of printing fabrics, and it too is relief printing.

Intaglio (pronounced in-tal-yo) printing is not quite so ancient, but it has been around for quite a while. When Rembrandt van Rijn printed one of his famous etchings, he used the intaglio process. *The image to be printed is*

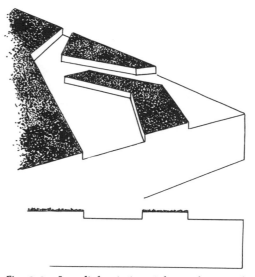

Fig. 2–2. In relief printing, ink on the raised sections of the printing plate is transferred by means of pressure to the surface being printed.

scratched with a needle or eaten with an acid below the surface of the printing plate. Ink is rubbed on the surface and worked into the fine etched or scratched line (Fig. 2–3). The surface of the plate is then wiped clean, but just as with the dirt around fingernails, it is almost impossible to wipe the ink out of those fine lines. The plate is then placed under a damp piece of paper and pressed very hard in a special etching press. Because of the pressure of the rollers and the softness of the damp paper, the paper is actually pressed right down into the troughs where it sucks up the ink, producing the print. One way

17

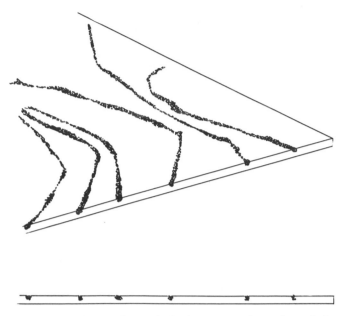

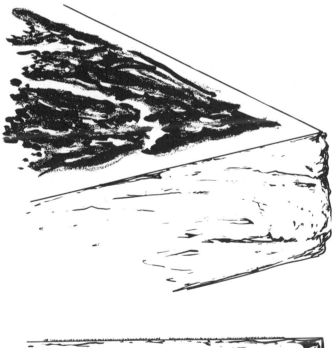

Fig. 2–3. In the intaglio method of printing, ink in the etched troughs of the printing plate is transferred with great pressure to the surface of the print.

Fig. 2–4. In planographic printing, the surface of the printing plate is flat. Sections to be printed are covered with a greasy substance to which ink adheres and the rest of the surface is dampened with water, which repels ink. The image is then transferred to the print surface.

to tell an intaglio print is to run your finger over the paper just a little outside the image area. You will find a slight ridge where the damp paper has been forced down over the outside edge of the printing plate. Some early fabric prints *(toile de Jouy)* using very fine lines were engraved on copper plates and printed by the intaglio method.

Planographic printing is more commonly known as lithography. *The printing image is neither raised in relief nor cut into the surface of the plate but is a treated area of the surface.* It works on the principle that water and grease will not mix but will resist each other (Fig. 2–4). The design is drawn or painted on the surface of a finely ground block of limestone—many commercial printers today use especially prepared metal plates—with a black greasy crayon or black greasy paint. The stone is then treated with gum arabic and nitric acid and dampened with water. When a large ink-charged roller is passed over the stone, the ink sticks to the greasy parts and is repelled by the wet areas. It is then put into a special press and printed. Many illustrations in magazines, posters, and children's books are printed in this manner, and some efforts have been made to print fabrics using this process. Photo-offset is another form of lithographic, or planographic, printing that is commonly used commercially.

Stencil printing (Fig. 2–5) is as old as relief printing. *The image is actually cut out of a thin material called a stencil, and printing ink is forced through the holes onto the surface to be printed.* The screen-process method that is the subject of this book is an important form of stencil printing.

Fig. 2–5. In stencil printing the ink is forced through holes in a material impervious to the ink (top) onto the surface being printed (bottom).

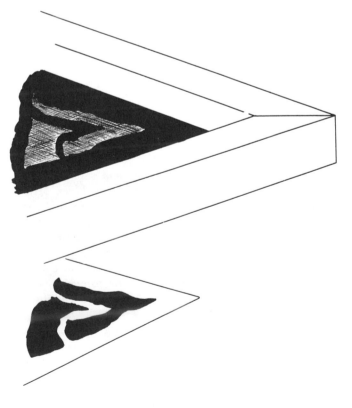

The screen-process stencil is an impervious material supported on a woven mesh (silk, linen, organdy, cotton, nylon, copper, bronze, brass, and stainless-steel fibers) tightly stretched on a rectangular frame. The secret of the process is that the stretched material both supports the stencil and prevents the semifluid paints or dye pastes from flowing easily through the stencil holes, yet when pressure is applied by means of a rubber squeegee pulled back and forth over the stencil, the paint or dye is forced through the woven mesh to produce the printed image.

The Screen-Process Print

Screen-process printing possesses amazing versatility. It is simple enough to be used by a child. It requires no elaborate workshop, no expensive presses, no unavailable inks or tools. In its rudimentary forms it can be easily and quickly mastered by an elementary-school class.

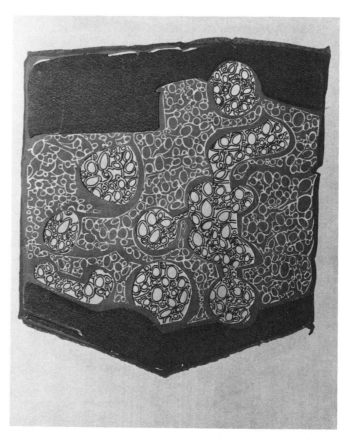

Fig. 2–7. (Reproduced in full color between pages 16 and 17.) The design for this serigraph, entitled "David's Shield," was drawn on transparent acetate and exposed on a light-sensitive emulsion resist. (By James A. Schwalbach)

Fig. 2–8. (Reproduced in full color between pages 16 and 17.) The fiber-reactive dye pastes used in this fabric print are easy to prepare. The designer has painted free, expressive lines after screen-printing the basic design, and where the two merge new colors are created. ("Purpled Scarf," by Irene Naik)

Yet, both the professional and the amateur who wish to explore the process in some depth will find it a rewarding challenge. It will print on almost any surface (glass, wood, paper, canvas, leather, fabric, stone—anything firm enough to hold the ink). While generally used on a flat surface, screens can be constructed to print on curved, round, or irregularly shaped forms. It is a portable process, and the frames can be moved wherever the artist chooses.

Screen printing allows the artist such a wide range of creative possibilities that it has become the most personal of all the printing processes. It inhibits the artist less than any other. The evolutionary growth of the printed image is completely under his control at every step. And contrary to all of the other methods of printing, it does not require him to make the mental translations of a reversed image.

He can make prints almost any size he wishes. He has at hand an extremely wide range of printing inks and dyes, either transparent, opaque, dull, shiny, or fluorescent. Some dry in minutes; others take hours. It is possible for him to build up textures and layers of paint so that he can achieve surfaces rich with color nuances or clear, cool, and flat or rhythmically calligraphic. They can be as fresh as a brush stroke that has scarcely dried. He can suit his approaches to a free, even abandoned and intuitive method or one as carefully controlled as a well-disciplined soldier. Many artists feel that screen-process printing is as versatile and personal as oil painting.

The stencil itself can be a very simple blockout scrubbed in with wax crayon by an eight-year-old child (see Chapter 3) or a very sophisticated halftone photographic image. The operation is basically small and simple, suited to a one-man kitchen-studio approach. But it has also become one of the giants of the commercial printing industry. (Large, complex, and automatic screen-process printing machines turn out 2,000 to 3,000 impressions every hour, all dried and neatly stacked, ready for packaging.) It prints articles as varied as advertising materials, banners, sweat shirts, dials for scientific instruments, electronic circuits for radio and television sets, labels on soda-pop bottles, designs on ceramic dishes, reproductions of oil paintings, yardgoods, wallpaper, and highway signs.

The Serigraph

To the professional or amateur artist, screen-process printing means the production of serigraphs, or original prints made by the screen-process printing method and produced by an artist after his own design for his own purpose.

In 1964 the Print Council of America defined an original print as follows:

"An original print is a work of art, the general requirements of which are: (1) The artist alone has created the master image in or upon the plate, stone, wood block or other material for the purpose of creating a print. (2) The print is made directly from the said material, by the artist or pursuant to his direction. (3) The finished print is approved by the artist."

When an artist makes a serigraph, he usually prints a definite number that he has decided in advance, or an edition of serigraphs. These are duplicates or near duplicates of the same master stencil. How precise the duplication is, is up to the individual artist. There will always be some variation among the prints in any one edition. However, a print that differs considerably from the others is not included in a signed edition. It may be saved and gain value as a unique print, especially if it is a good one. Occasionally an artist holds on to prints produced during the evolution of the edition. These generally differ somewhat from the edition and are either destroyed or labeled "proof prints." Prints that do not come up to the standards of the artist are also destroyed.

Screen-Process Textile Printing

When you think of the quantities of fabrics printed by large textile plants that specialize in roller printing, you might be tempted to qualify all fabrics produced by the screen-process method as fine art. Yet there are many large manufacturers that use semiautomatic screen-process printing machines to print rather large quantities of fabric. Since many of these employ excellent designers, the fabrics are hard to distinguish from the product of a small hand-process studio. But both have an advantage over the much larger roller-printing industry. In screen-process printing there is more penetration of the color into the fibers of the fabric, which results in stronger, more vivid colors. Also, the screen-process industry, especially the smaller workshops, can afford to be a little more experimental and daring. They generally have lower investment in equipment and print smaller runs that involve a lower market risk. Many of the smaller workshops specialize in high-quality fabrics of distinctive design for such specialty markets as high-fashion apparel construction.

It should be mentioned that the printing of better wallpaper is similar to screen-process fabric printing, and most of the information in this book concerning fabrics applies equally to wallpaper.

Basically there are three methods of printing a design in or on a piece of fabric: direct, discharge, and resist. In the *direct* process the color is printed directly through the holes in the process stencil onto the surface of the cloth. In the *discharge* process the cloth is dyed before it is printed. A paste containing a bleaching agent is then printed on the cloth through the holes of the process stencil. This bleach paste selectively bleaches the dyed cloth, producing a design that is lighter than the dyed cloth. The *resist* process is somewhat similar to the dis-

Fig. 2–6.   Stretching a screen fabric on a printing frame is tricky. The screen must be very tight so that no sags can develop.

charge process. A specially prepared paste is printed on the cloth through the holes of the process stencil, causing the printed areas to resist dye. The cloth is then placed in a dye solution. The design is also lighter than the dyed background.

Fabric design presents an entirely different problem from that facing serigraphers. Fabrics are usually continuous lengths of cloth, and the design must continue as long as the cloth does. Therefore the design must work visually in all directions, or at least in two directions. Often a unit of a design that is to be repeated looks one way when it stands alone, but when it is repeated in one or more directions, it takes on an entirely different character. Certain parts of the unit that do not predominate (these parts frequently are near the outside edges of the unit) will join forces with sympathetic parts in the next unit and gain strength in the union. This can produce either a very dynamic design or one that falls apart because of conflicting forces.

Movement or rhythm produced visually is a very important part of textile design. Some interesting analogies can be made with music. In music there is a repetition of simple motifs of sound as there is a repetition of single visual motifs in fabric design. This will cause certain configurations of sound in music and certain configurations of pattern in fabric design. This unifies the pattern into a continuing design that is the lifeblood of the entire product and gives a vitality to the design that is difficult to get in a more static art.

Another musical analogy can be made. Music is performed by different individuals, and therefore there are slight variations from one performance to another as each musician interprets the sound configurations of the composer. A somewhat similar thing happens in the hand-printing of a fabric design. For no human being can work in exactly the same way each time he prints one of the design units on the fabric. The pressure of the squeegee

is changed slightly; the paint is changed slightly in hue or consistency; the screen is placed a very small fraction of an inch out of line. These add a personal touch to the configuration planned for the design and a vitality that one cannot find even in the screen-process prints produced by semiautomatic machines and that certainly is absent in roller-printed fabrics.

It is the interesting, creative textile printer who carefully and deliberately seeks such a random effect in the printing process. Often certain changes of color can be made as each unit is printed. This must be done with great sensitivity, for it is usually only one small step away from catastrophic disorganization and aesthetic failure.

The fabric designer is also presented with an unknown that can easily complicate his problem. The appearance of the printed fabric as a dress or draperies is usually far different from its appearance on the printing table. Fab-

Fig. 2–9. A scooper cutter, or scratch tool, is a versatile instrument in making a cut-film stencil. The fine lines in this fabric' print inspired by Pennsylvania Dutch designs would be very difficult if not impossible without such a tool. ("Zoorama," by Alta Hertzler)

rics are all printed flat but hardly ever used flat, and a design must be able to follow the folds and drapes of the materials and still maintain its quality. If the design is to be cut apart, rearranged, and pieced together into clothing, creative and careful planning is called for. Many fabrics are used as support or background for other activities. A tablecloth, for example, is designed to protect the table and to make the meal more pleasant and possibly even more palatable. A tablecloth design that competes with the meal and dishes might be a most unhappy one.

Where Do You Get Your Ideas and What Do You Do with Them?

While screen-process printing may be fun and recreation, do not count on it and do not seek this from it. For any serious pursuit of a creative process requires concentration, absorption, and intensity of purpose. It is a job that requires full creative and intellectual attention. What started out in fun may turn out to be blood and sweat if it is to amount to anything worthwhile. There is no magic way to do it. There is no doctrine. Success lies in being flexible and trying different approaches, methods, and ideas. All we can do is suggest some ideas that might start your thinking in a useful direction.

Basically there are two different ways that you can approach the design problem in screen-process printing. You can work intuitively, feeling your way, allowing the material and the process to suggest what to do next. This is an attitude that well suits the personalities of some designers. It gives you a chance to make use of happy accidents, providing, of course, that you are sensitive and knowledgeable enough to recognize a happy accident when you see it. Many designers are disturbed by any kind of accident and cannot differentiate between the unfortunate and the fortunate ones. The intuitive approach is probably a good one for most neophyte screen-process designers to take because it tends to keep your ideas more compatible with the process. Your final print is more likely to be suited to the screen process if you let the process dictate the major directions the design should take. However, when designers work intuitively there comes a critical moment when the seeming chaos must be organized into some kind of valid, clear statement. Some control must be exercised at this point. Many designers do not recognize this moment until the design has become hopelessly lost. Others find themselves incapable of exercising the control necessary to solidify the design.

After some experience with the materials and tools, most (but not all) designers work best if they get some sort of a general notion beforehand about the design they would like to produce. This can be done with sketches. If he wants, the designer can break up a sketch into its various color components and paint each one on different pieces of clear acetate or tracing paper. These then are

Fig. 2–10. The hairband above is printed with chiaroscuro made with a film line cutter (scooper cutter or scratch tool) in Profilm. In the radiating motif below, semitransparent white ink is printed on dark fabric with a lacquer stencil. The artist designed the pattern with free brush strokes of lacquer applied directly to the screen fabric. (Hairband by Joy H. Dohr; radiating motif by Gretchen Widder)

placed over each other, and some approximation of the final design can be visualized. Changes will suggest themselves even before the printing begins. Generally it is better to simplify designs rather than complicate them. But however the sketch appears, it can only approximate the final print. The designer must be quite willing to make changes, even drastic ones, as the print evolves.

Serigraphers will need to think of the total area within the design unit. It is easy to think of the positive forms that are printed, but we tend to forget negative unprinted space around and behind these positive forms. This is an equally important part of the visual statement and should be given equally careful consideration. A good screen print allows the background to take shape and become an integral part of the motif. In addition, fabric designers should use acetates, tissue paper, or carbons to repeat their design units in as many different directions as is necessary in order to get some idea how the units will interrelate and how the visual statement will be affected by that interrelation. Units can be interconnected with many

devices, a few of which are: (1) a side-by-side continuous pattern; (2) sinuous and expressive lines that extend from one unit into the next in one or more directions; (3) negative space that creates a similar directional fluidity; (4) notches from one irregular unit that carefully fit into reverse notches in the adjoining irregular unit. Connections may need to be both vertical and horizontal in fabric designing. Often a rhythm or concealed beat can be injected into a fabric design by carefully created breaks or fractures between the various units.

But besides form, line, and texture, screen printing is most importantly an expression in color, and color experience can be gained only in the process of printing. The material on which the color is printed has a great deal to do with the final effect of the color. The amount of opac-

Fig. 2–11. Knotted yarn, paper clips, and small rubber bands were used to create this design. To make the resist the artist arranged these objects directly on a light-sensitive emulsion and exposed the emulsion. (By Mathilda V. Schwalbach)

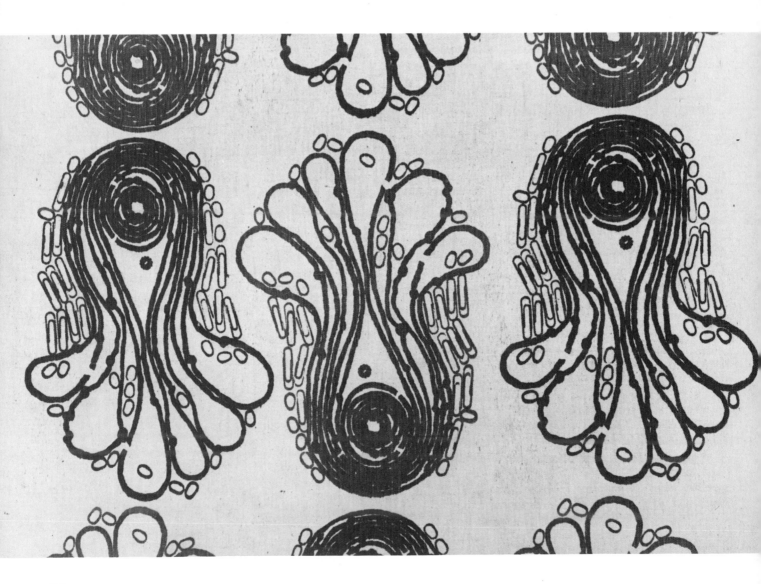

ity and transparency of each color used is also critical. Since certain effects can be achieved by overprinting colors, most of the colors used will have certain qualities of transparency and each color can be evaluated only after it has been printed over the color underneath.

Man can consciously and intuitively control his visual forms, and much can be learned from his environment, particularly his natural environment. For in nature there is an inexhaustible resource of ideas. Serious designers should carry small sketchbooks with them for recording ideas, for both serigraph and textile-design ideas have a habit of unpredictable genesis.

Because of the prominence of the camera in our contemporary experience and because of its heavy use in television, our society is becoming more and more visually oriented. So the younger you are, the more visually acute you probably are.

A successful designer or artist is able to individualize his visual language. A Paul Klee is a marvelous colorist and a witty and delightfully surprising designer . . . an Henri Matisse is bold and strong in his flat color abstractions . . . a Piet Mondriaan is orderly and meticulous with his geometric patterns . . . a Ben Shahn is socially perceptive and both witty and caustic in his calligraphic line quality. But no one else has been exactly like any of them, and no one will be exactly like any successful fabric designer or serigrapher. His visual signature will be recognizably his own. This is the very difficult but necessary goal that the serious designer must set for himself. It comes only after long experience and many trials and errors in a never-ending search.

The Possibilities and Limitations of Materials and Tools

New ideas and new techniques are always thrilling and exciting, and it is natural that the first thrills and experiences in screen printing will be related almost completely to techniques, tools, and materials. This stage must be passed through as quickly as possible, for it is not until the technique of the craft becomes second nature that any significant prints or designs are likely to result.

Each craft and art form has its own peculiar attributes and limitations. Screen-process printing is no exception. But there is no way that anyone can give you an understanding of them. There is an experience that must be and can be acquired only by working with the materials, tools, and processes involved. Work must be extensive enough to make experience intuitive. It must become second nature. It must become an easily functioning part of the designer's creative vocabulary.

The major materials are paper and fabric, paint and dye. Both are different from each other and different from anything else. Paper is flat and usually white and smooth, but not always so. Fabrics have a peculiar flexibility that must be understood and used. Rarely does a serigraph look like a fabric or a fabric like a serigraph.

The whole study of dyes and paints is a gargantuan task that certainly is beyond the scope of any individual printer. But minimum characteristics of the visual and chemical reactions must be learned. It is exciting when a serigrapher or fabric designer sees what happens with his first color overprinting. What unexpected variety there is in the ways colors will dry as they are printed on different surfaces with varying degrees of penetration.

When the serigrapher or fabric designer knows his process well enough to be able to anticipate its actions, then he can really begin to design intelligently and significantly.

Significant Expression Relates to a Living Contemporary Culture

The humanist philosopher, Kenneth L. Patton, in *Man Is the Meaning*, said: "His [man's] body is the bed of a stream through which flow the many waters of his world and his race. A man is many wires strung in the wind, and he must sing the song of the air that flows over him." Meaningful expression grows out of the culture in which it is rooted. This has always been understood by artists and designers of significance.

Today swift communication and transportation have shrunk not only our world but our universe as well. The electron microscope and other scientific marvels have given us fresh new looks at our environment. We are becoming more conscious of social and political inequities —of injustice and human strife. François Bucher, in his book, *Josef Albers: Despite Straight Lines*, stated: "Rapid motion within seemingly stable systems has changed our daily way of life as well as our inner imagery. We sit in a car or in a plane while the landscape slips by. Rocks change their shape, rivers and roads change their course relative to our eyes. Façades rise while we approach, recede and decline while we go by. Matter, the matrix of being, has become a function of energy and its dynamic and infinite transformations."

Man has always spoken of his culture through the arts, and relevant serigraphy and textile design will continue to be responsive to these cultural forces. There are also social implications to creative activity, especially that kind of creative studio experience that involves more than one person. For within the necessary freedom of the creative studio environment, true individualism can flower only in an atmosphere of sensitive mutual respect and understanding of each individual's efforts. The artist must learn the difficult procedures of both self- and group evaluation, for without continued scrutiny and evaluation no progress is possible. There is a kind of freedom of expression that can be practical only within the social and utilitarian demands of a group studio experience, and it is a very healthy experience psychologically for the participants.

3. A PRINT FOR THE BEGINNER

Because the rudiments of screen-process printing are simple, Johnny can become a serigrapher and give up jam printing.

Using cardboard frames and squeegee, organdy screen, paper stencils, and conditioned school tempera paint, elementary silk-screen prints can be produced. Let's follow the process step by step.

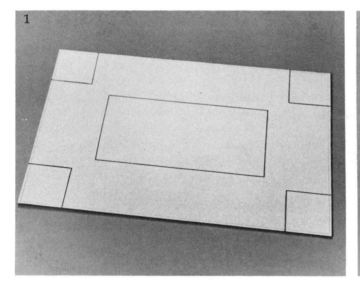

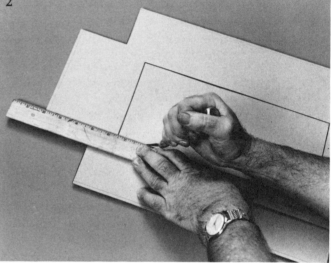

Step 1. With a ruler, measure carefully a rectangle of stiff cardboard (you can use a shoebox) for the construction of a printing-frame box. Measurements, of course, will be determined by the size of the prints you want to make, but suggested measurements for your first box are: 13 by 21 inches for the size of the cardboard, 3 by 3 inches for the corner squares and 5 by 12 inches for the size of the centered printing rectangle or hole.

Step 2. On a smooth, hard surface that you cannot damage (a piece of Masonite or another piece of cardboard is excellent), cut out the corners and the centered rectangle in your piece of cardboard.

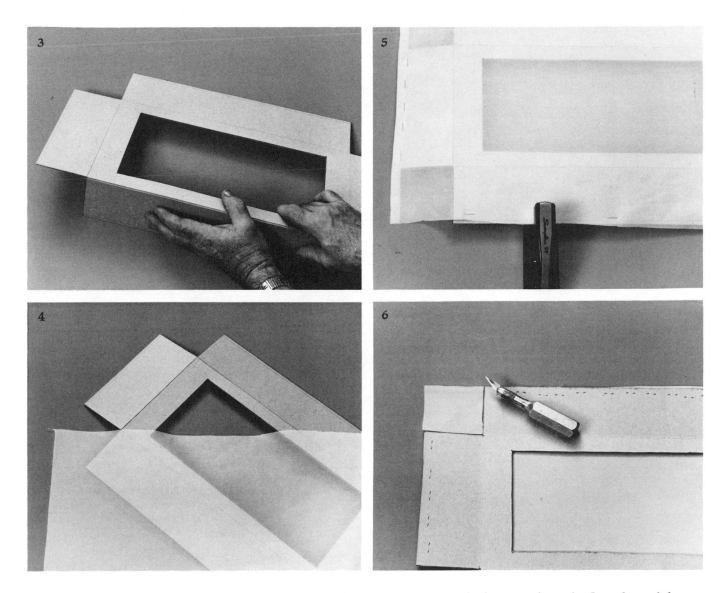

Step 3. Score the outside edge of the fold on the cardboard with a dull knife or scissor blade. This gives you a clean, sharp folded edge.

Step 4. Cut a piece of ordinary cotton organdy the exact size of the outside edge of your piece of cut cardboard. If the cardboard is 13 by 21 inches, the piece of organdy should be 13 by 21 inches.

Step 5. Staple the organdy to the flap edges of the unfolded cardboard on what will be the outside of the box, and pull the organdy snug but not too tight. Folding the sides up to form the box frame (Step 7) will tighten the organdy just the proper amount.

Step 6. With a sharp stencil knife or pair of scissors, cut out or remove the excess organdy at each of the four corners.

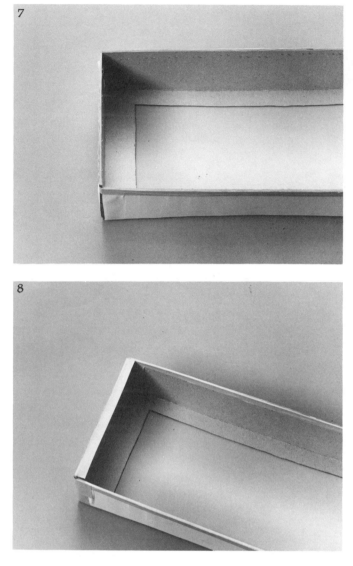

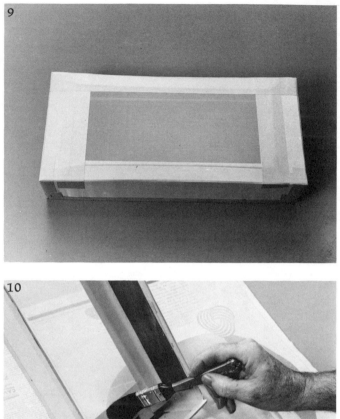

Step 7. Carefully fold up the sides of the cardboard to form the box. The organdy will be stretched tightly over the outside of the box. Hold the box sides in place with a piece of masking tape running around the entire outside of the box just at the top edge.

Step 8. Protect the upper edges of the box with masking tape—seal all four corners both inside and outside. Put masking tape over all folded edges of the cardboard both inside and out to be sure it does not leak. *Note:* If masking tape is not available, heavy gummed paper tape may be used, but it is a little more difficult to handle.

Step 9. Also use masking tape around all four sides of the rectangular hole both inside and outside of the box, extending the tape so that it covers about 1/4 inch of the organdy over the hole inside and out. This is very important to ensure clean printing. It will help prevent the paint from blurring and running around the outside edges. The cardboard used is generally too thick to give the squeegee good contact with the printing surfaces at the outside edges. This procedure reduces that thickness to a workable point.

Step 10. Using ordinary finishing lacquer or shellac, paint the entire inside of the box. Include all of the taped areas, but be careful to get *no* lacquer or shellac on the organdy. One coat will suffice but, if you wish, a second coat will give better protection.

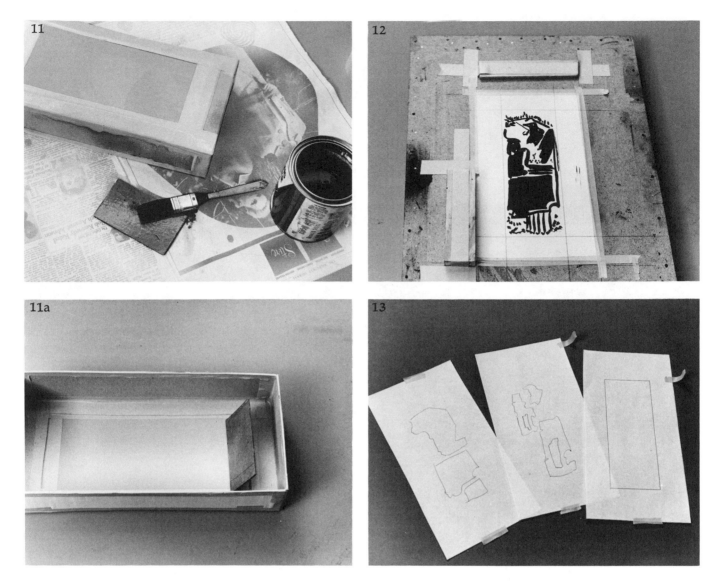

Step 11. Cover the outside area of the box with one or two coats of lacquer or shellac in a similar fashion. For a squeegee, cut a piece of very stiff cardboard that will fit exactly within the printing hole in the box frame. If it is not stiff enough, two or more identical pieces should be glued together. The printing edge of the cardboard piece (the part that rests against the organdy in the photo) must be as straight as possible to minimize printing problems. Coat this cardboard piece heavily with several coats of shellac or lacquer on both sides. The box and the squeegee are now ready for printing.

Step 12. Tape the proposed sketch of the final print to a printing board (which can be a flat piece of Masonite or plywood or a table top). Draw lines on the sketch to in-dicate the outer limits of the printing hole in the card-board printing box. Then tape a block of wood at the top of the board and one on the left side that will be flush with the top and left side of printing box. This is a simple way to key prints, and several colors can then be printed over each other.

Note: The following steps show how to print five colors together, but it might be wise to limit your first serigraph to one color.

Step 13. Three stencils have been placed over the sketch (see photo, Step 12) and traced. Ordinary news-print can be used. Use carbon paper or temporarily re-move the original sketch from the printing board and place it on a window against the light so you can see the design. The stencil on the right will be a solid background color; stencil two (center) will be color forms in the sec-ond printing; and stencil three (far left) will be used for the third color; the cutout scraps will form the designs for the fourth color.

Step 14. Cut the stencils with a sharp razor blade or a stencil knife on a smooth surface that you cannot damage. Save the individual parts that are cut out for printing the fourth color.

Step 15. With masking tape, place two keying tabs at the left side of the printing area and two at the top side. This will ensure that the printing paper is positioned accurately for the printing of each color.

Step 16. Place the paper stencil over the sketch and place the printing box over the stencil in the proper position. Temporarily fasten the stencil in place on the outside of the printing box over the organdy screen with mucilage.

Step 17. Lay the first sheet of printing paper carefully under the four keying tabs. Number the upper left-hand corner of the sheet to ensure that the paper is inserted properly with each color printing.

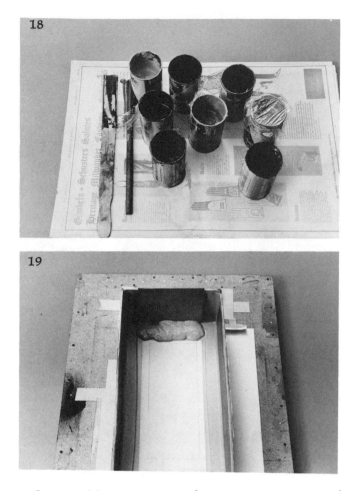

Step 18. Mix your paint to the proper consistency and transparency (you will have to experiment a bit with the consistency). Small cans are very convenient for this. Oil paint that is left over can be stored for long periods if a bit of paint thinner or turpentine is floated on top and the can covered with a piece of plastic food wrapping. The plastic wrapping is sealed with wet paint and held in place with a rubber band. Clear plastic allows you to inspect the color without breaking the seal.

The paint used in these photographs is traditional oil-based screen-process paint purchased from a commercial supplier. If you are making your first prints, however, the following paint formula, which is easier to use and clean, is recommended: to 1 1/2 cups of water add enough powdered tempera paint to produce a consistency like very heavy coffee cream; then add 1 teaspoon of soap flakes and 2 teaspoons of glycerin (available at your local drugstore).

Step 19. Place a small amount of the mixed paint in one end of the printing box. Avoid getting any of the paint in the screen hole. Put the box on the printing area with the top end and the left side up against the wooden key blocks. Always place the box in exactly the same position. You may wish to mark one end as the top to identify it easily.

Step 20. Scrape the paint from one end of the box to the other, pulling the cardboard squeegee carefully and firmly. Then lift up the box, remove the printing paper, and put in a new sheet of paper. Again put the cardboard printing box down in position and turn the cardboard squeegee around (do not turn the printing box around). Turning the squeegee with each print keeps all the ink on one side of the squeegee and gives a cleaner, more uniform print. Pull the squeegee back the other way, pulling the paint over the second sheet of paper. Repeat this process until the desired number of papers have the first color area printed on them. Carefully remove the paper stencil from the box and then remove the paint. Thoroughly clean the organdy screen and the squeegee with turpentine or paint thinner for oil-based paint; water for the tempera paint.

Step 21. Repeat Steps 16 through 20 with the second paper stencil to print the second color.

Step 22. Repeat Steps 16 through 20 with stencil three to print color area three.

Step 23. Place stencil three (see photo in Step 13) on the key drawing again. Then arrange the individual bits cut from this stencil in position. (They have been trimmed somewhat so they no longer completely fill the hole they were cut from.) Carefully place the cardboard printing box in position over the sketch. Lightly glue (with a water-soluble glue or mucilage) the various pieces to the screen mesh, using little dabs of glue pressed through the mesh. When the glue has dried, lift up the printing box. The small pieces of paper from the paper stencil will be temporarily fastened to the silk.

Step 24. After the glue has dried on the meshes, lift the box and remove the original sketch. Replace it with a piece of scrap paper, and print the color over the scrap paper. The stickiness of the printing ink will affix the smaller paper stencil parts to the mesh more firmly. Now print the fourth color on each sheet of paper (see Step 20).

Step 25. Place the screen mesh on the original sketch. Lightly pencil in areas that might comprise the next color to be printed. Lift the box off the sketch and, with lacquer, shellac, or glue, paint in on the organdy those areas that are *not* to be printed.

Step 26. After the lacquer, shellac, or glue has dried, put ink in the frame and print the fifth color on each sheet of paper (see Step 20). This will complete the edition of prints. You can see in the progression of color photographs what a print looks like after each of the five colors has been added.

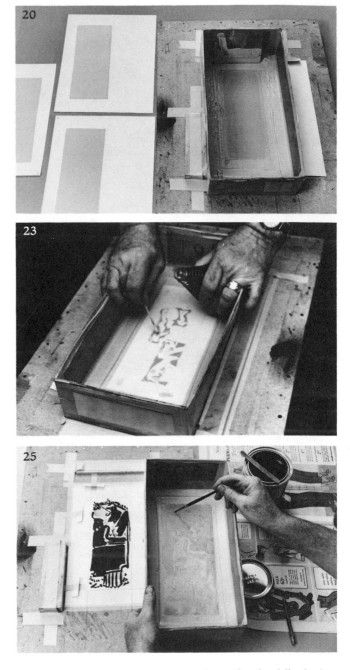

The illustrations on the facing page are all reproduced in full color between pages 16 and 17.

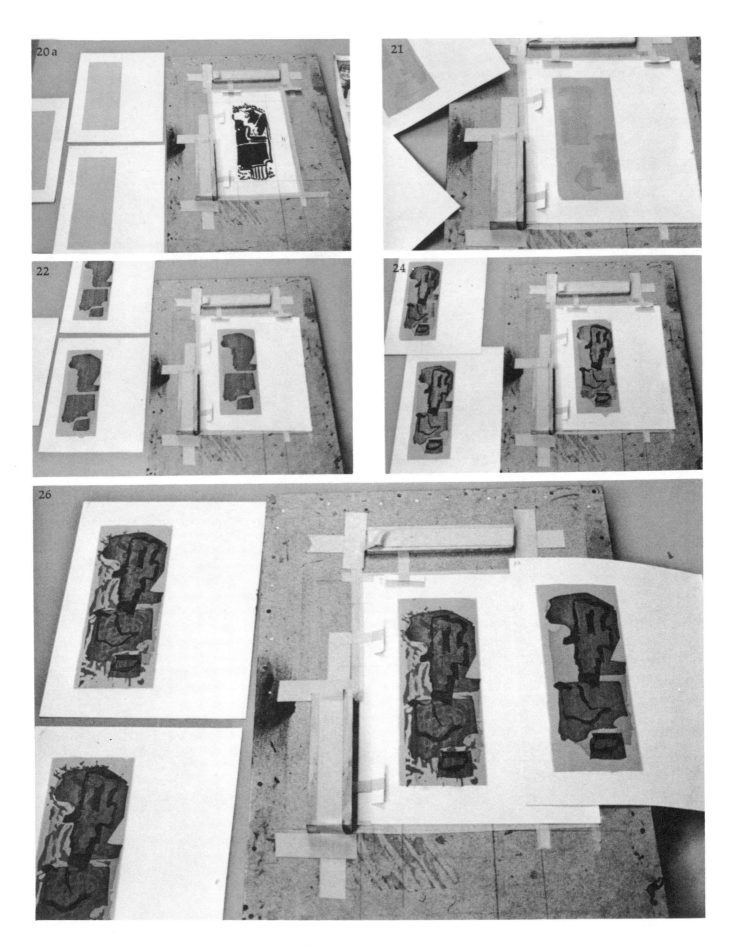

Another Variation. A very easy method for making a one-color textile print is to draw the design directly on the organdy with any color wax crayon. Press hard on the crayon to fill the meshes with wax, working against a smooth, hard surface so that the screen remains taut. Then print with the tempera paint mixture previously described, or another water-based textile ink. It is best to do this with only one color since the wax crayon design is very difficult to remove from the screen. Print every other unit first, and then go back and print the missing units.

4. PRODUCING A SERIGRAPH STEP BY STEP

While the screen printing process can be used by a child with the most elementary means, the basic printing frame and other materials needed by the artist a few years older than Johnny are more difficult to construct and use. Let us now follow, step by step, the production of two different wooden printing frames and the printing of a five-color print using three different stencil resists. If you are producing your first print, it might be wise to limit yourself to one color until you get the feel of the process.

Two Wooden Printing Frames

A simple butt-joint frame. Cut four pieces of lumber. For a small frame, 1- by 2-inch clear pine can be used; for larger frames use 2- by 2-inch lumber. Edges should be cut precisely square and the width of the long pieces should be marked on the ends of the small pieces to make the assembly job more accurate (Fig. 4–2). The size of the frame will depend on the size of the print you wish to produce. Inside measurements should be 3 inches wider and 6 inches longer than the desired print size.

Construct the wooden frame (Fig. 4–3) with a simple butt joint, nailing the ends together with 3- to 4-inch finishing nails. Be very careful because, when assembled, the frame must lie flat on the printing table surface. Use

Fig. 4–1. These wooden printing frames are in various stages of use. The young man on the left is putting the finishing touches on a frame he is making, in the center ink is being mixed for a print in progress, and at right the serigrapher is painting a resist on the screen.

Fig. 4–2. Lumber is cut to size for a frame made with a butt joint and the width of the long pieces is marked on the ends of the short pieces.

Fig. 4–3. The butt-joint frame is ready for nailing.

glue in the joints if desired, and attach a metal angle iron on the top side of each corner to strengthen the joints of larger frames (Fig. 4–4).

Stretch a piece of silk-screen silk over the underside of the wooden frame with a staple gun (Fig. 4–5), or small tacks if a stapler is not available. Organdy will work if the frame is to be used only a few times. Nylon should

Fig. 4–4. Angle irons are screwed over each butt joint to strengthen the frame at the corners.

Fig. 4–5. A staple gun is used to fasten the screen fabric to the frame.

Fig. 4–6. Lacquer or shellac painted on the screen where it contacts the wood ensures a secure bond.

Fig. 4–7. The outside of the frame should be sealed with masking or gummed tape.

Fig. 4–8. For a good seal the tape is extended down over the outside of the frame.

be put on frames to be used with a photo stencil. Start at the center of each side and work from left to right and from one side to the other. Finish the two opposite sides before you start on the remaining two sides. Stretch the cloth as tightly as possible, virtually to the point of tearing it. Keep the weave pattern parallel to the sides of the frame. The tension should be as uniform as you can make it.

Brush clear finishing lacquer or shellac on the cloth where it comes in contact with the wooden edge of the frame (Fig. 4–6). This ensures an even, secure adhesion of the cloth and helps to prevent leaking. Allow the lacquer or shellac to dry before the next step.

Seal the outside edges of the frame with at least two strips of gummed or masking tape around all four sides (Fig. 4–7). Extend the tape over the cloth about 1 inch and extend it down the side of the frame about 1 inch (Fig. 4–8).

Fig. 4–9. The tape and the outside of the frame need at least one coat of lacquer or shellac for protection.

Fig. 4–10. The inside of the frame must also be sealed with tape.

Fig. 4–11. The inside of the frame and the tape also should be protected with at least one coat of lacquer or shellac.

Fig. 4–12. A drop-pin hinge is used to attach the frame to its base.

With clear finishing lacquer or shellac, brush the tape and the outside of the frame with at least one coat (Fig. 4–9). Although not necessary, two coats are even better. Be careful not to get any lacquer or shellac on the open mesh of the cloth.

Seal the inside of the printing frame with at least one strip of gummed or masking tape (Fig. 4–10). Again extend the tape about 1 inch over the cloth and a similar distance up the side of the frame. Be sure the tape adheres evenly, since humps will make printing more difficult.

Also be very careful to see that the tape comes up tight into the corners.

Now brush clear finishing lacquer or shellac over the tape on the inside of the frame (Fig. 4–11). One coat will suffice, but two would be better. Again be very careful not to get any of the lacquer or shellac on the open mesh of the cloth. Taping and sealing with lacquer or shellac prevent paint leakage during the printing process. The frame is now ready to be fastened to the printing board.

Using two drop-pin hinges with small screws, attach

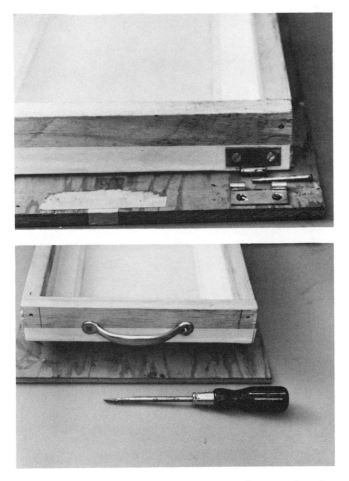

Fig. 4–13. If the male and female parts of the hinge on the other side of the frame are reversed, several different frames can be fastened to the same pair of hinges on the printing board with a minimum investment in hardware (see Fig. 7–5 in Chapter 7).

Fig. 4–14. An ordinary screen-door handle on the opposite end of the frame from the hinges facilitates raising the screen.

the frame to a very flat, smooth piece of plywood or to Masonite (Figs. 4–12 and 4–13). The printing board should extend beyond the outside edges of the frame by an inch or more on all sides. The center pin of a drop-pin hinge can be pushed out, making it possible to remove the frame from the printing board to change stencils and clean the frame between the printing of each color.

With small screws, fasten an inexpensive screen-door handle (Fig. 4–14) to the outside edge of the printing frame on the opposite end from the hinges.

Fig. 4–15. A wooden leg makes a good prop for the screen when it must be raised for any period of time.

Fig. 4–16. The frame is completely assembled and ready for printing.

Fig. 4–17. The pieces of frame lumber are assembled and glued at the corners.

Fig. 4–18. The joints of the frame are secured with corrugated fasteners after being glued.

Fasten a short length of wood to one side of the printing frame (Fig. 4–15). First, drill a hole in one end of the piece of wood, then insert a large screw eye through this hole and screw it into one side of the frame near the handle end until the piece of wood is tight. The screw eye allows you to tighten or loosen the piece of wood, which serves to prop the screen up off the printing paper when desired. The frame is now finished and ready for printing (Fig. 4–16).

A grooved frame with mitered corners. The lengths desired for the frame should be cut and mitered at each end and a groove 1/8 inch wide and 3/8 inch deep cut in the center of the underside of each of the four pieces of wood. The printer can do this himself in a home workshop if he has the skill. Some lumber companies will do it for a small charge. Prepared and precut pieces of wood can be purchased from many screen-process supply houses.

On a flat, solid surface place the four pieces of wood together to form the frame (Fig. 4–17). Use glue at the joints.

Hammer a corrugated fastener across the diagonal cut of each corner miter on one side (Fig. 4–18), then turn the frame over and repeat the process in the four corners on the other side. Be very careful that the wood does not split. Make absolutely sure that the fasteners on the side of the frame that contains the groove are flush with the

Fig. 4–19. The screen fabric is stretched over the frame and lightly fixed in place by the cord, which is hammered into the groove at intervals around the frame.

Fig. 4–20. Proper screen tension is achieved by pounding the cord deeper into the groove.

surface of the wood. This will be the printing side of the frame, and nothing must protrude from it. It is desirable to strengthen each of the corners with long finishing nails pounded in from the ends. On very large frames, attach metal corner braces on the side away from the groove for added strength (see Fig. 4–4). When assembled, the frame must lie absolutely flat on the printing surface.

Place the screen fabric (organdy for frames used only once; silk if desired; nylon for frames used with photographic stencils) over the grooved side of the frame. Fix the fabric in place temporarily by pounding a cord (about the thickness of venetian-blind cord) with a hammer into the groove every 2 inches or so all the way around (Fig. 4–19). Work from one side to the other to keep the fabric

stretched as evenly as possible. Screen-process supply companies sell 100-foot rolls of cord especially designed for this purpose.

With a hammer and a blunt piece of metal no thicker than 1/8 inch, or a large screwdriver, carefully force the cord down into the groove. This will tighten the fabric to a very high tension (Fig. 4–20). Screen-process supply companies sell a tool especially designed for this step. If you make many frames, it will be useful to own one.

Now seal the frame with tape and lacquer, and fasten it to the printing board as described in Chapter 3.

Fig. 4–21.   The first paper stencil—in this case for a solid background color—is cut after it is traced from the prepared sketch and taped in place on the printing board as a guide.

Fig. 4–22.   Metal keying tabs position paper more accurately than paper tabs.

Fig. 4–23.   The stencil for the first color is lightly taped to the printing frame in position for printing.

Fig. 4–24.   A rubber squeegee is a more satisfactory tool than a cardboard squeegee.

Printing a Five-Color Serigraph Using Three Different Resists to Produce the Final Print

Colors one, two, and three—paper stencils. These are made and used in exactly the same manner as the paper stencils in Chapter 3. The prepared sketch is taped in place on the printing board and the first paper stencil is traced and cut (Fig. 4–21). The masking tape keying tabs described in Chapter 3 can be used here to make sure that the printing paper is always placed on the printing board in the proper place. But metal tabs (Fig. 4–22) are more accurate and convenient. Position the first stencil (Fig. 4–23) and tape it to the frame ready for printing (see Chapter 3, Step 16).

Now place some screen-process paint in one end of the frame and pull it from one side of the frame to the other with a rubber squeegee (Fig. 4–24). Then pick up the excess ink with the squeegee and return it to the far end of the frame. Try to keep all of the paint on one side of the rubber blade of the squeegee to get a clean, even color. The print can be changed slightly by varying the pressure used on the squeegee. The squeegee should be held at about a 60-degree angle for best results.

When all of the prints of the edition have the first color printed on them, scoop up the excess paint with a rubber spatula (Fig. 4–25) and return it to the paint can for future use. Cover the paint with a thin coating of turpentine or paint thinner and seal the open can end with clear plastic (see Chapter 3, Step 18). Clean the frame very thoroughly with turpentine or paint thinner.

Fig. 4–25. A rubber spatula is excellent for scraping paint off the squeegee and the frame.

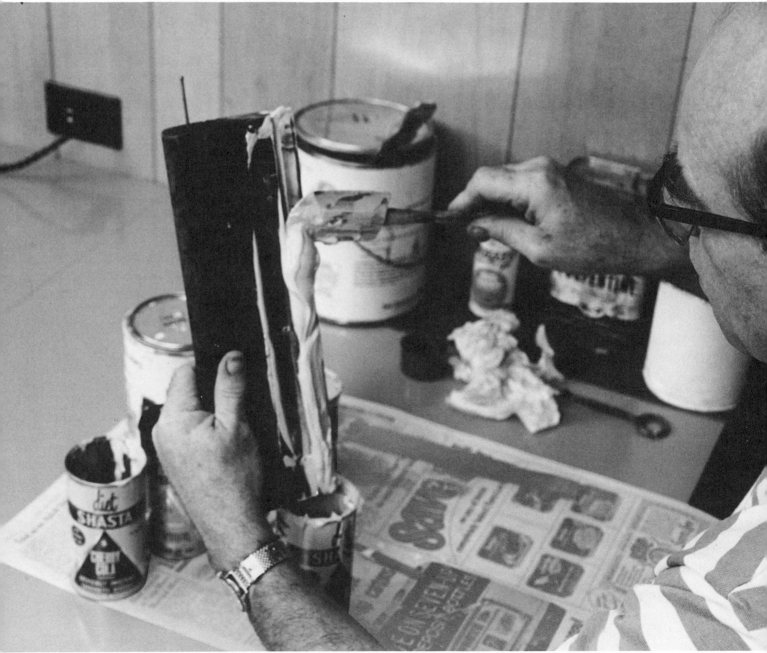

Repeat these instructions for the second (Fig. 4–26) and third colors.

Color four—lacquer-film stencil. For the fourth color, you can obtain from screen-process supply companies specially prepared lacquer-film stencils and a scooper cutter, which are used for very hard, sharply defined color areas and reasonably fine lines. The lacquer stencil consists of two layers of material: a lower support layer of heavy, transparent wax paper under a very thin coat of lightly tinted lacquer. The scooper cutter is a special kind of stencil knife with a small sharp loop of metal that does the cutting. It is excellent for getting a sketchy line in a lacquer-film stencil (Scooper cutters are available in three different sizes; see Fig. 4–27).

Place the lacquer film over the original sketch for the print and, using a scooper cutter, cut any fine lines in the lacquer film (Fig. 4–28). Areas that are to print solid with hard edges are now cut out with a very sharp stencil knife. It pays to keep one knife blade to use exclusively for this step. There should be as little pressure on the blade as possible. It is important to cut only the thin top

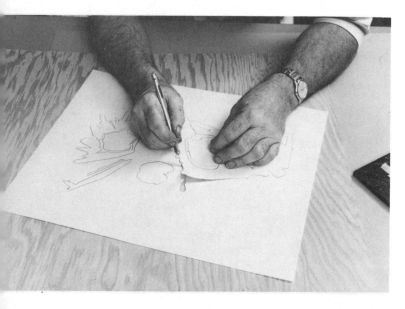

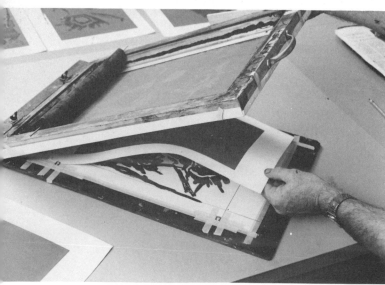

Fig. 4–27. Besides the ordinary single-blade stencil cutter (left), three sizes of scooper cutters are used to cut lacquer film.

Fig. 4–28. Scooper cutters make fine lines in lacquer-film stencils, while stencil cutters are used for cutting out solid areas.

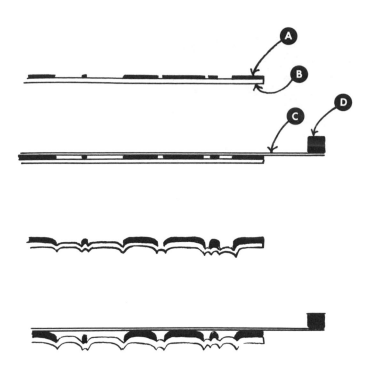

Fig. 4–29. The top two parts of the drawing show the results of proper pressure on the knife in cutting a lacquer-film stencil. *A* is the lacquer film that remains after cutting, and *B* is the protective wax-paper backing. In the second cross section the screen fabric (*C*) has been adhered to the film with lacquer solvent; note the perfectly flat contact between the two. *D* is the wooden edge of the printing frame. The bottom two parts show what happens when the pressure on the cutting knife is too heavy. The knife has bent the wax-paper backing at the edge of each area of film so that when the screen fabric (the flat part in the bottom cross section) is adhered the bent wax paper prevents the edges of the lacquer film from making contact with it.

layer of colored lacquer, *not* the wax paper (see Fig. 4–29); in fact, do not even bend the wax paper. Too much pressure may not cut through the wax paper, but it may be just enough to bend the paper, which will cause difficulties when it comes to adhering the lacquer film to the screen. Bent wax paper will prevent the cut edges of the lacquer film from properly contacting the screen.

Outline a solid area with a light touch of your sharp stencil knife, then pick up an edge of the area and carefully peel it off the wax paper (Fig. 4–30). As the stencil progresses, you can see the design develop because the light color in the lacquer film contrasts with the white of the wax paper.

Adhering a cut lacquer-film stencil to the screen fabric takes the most skill in this process. Because the film of lacquer is very thin, it is easy to use too much lacquer thinner or film adherent and dissolve the stencil completely. Work cautiously at first.

After you cut the stencil, position it in the proper place under the printing frame over the sketch (which was fastened in place on the printing board before the first color was printed). The lacquer side is in contact with the fabric mesh, and the wax paper side is down. There are two parts to this step that must follow each other very quickly. First, rub a small rag, rather heavily saturated with lacquer thinner (or film adherent), lightly and for only a few seconds over a small section of the screen fabric on the inside of the printing frame, wetting both the fabric and the lacquer film underneath (Fig. 4–31). *Immediately* press a large, dry rag quickly on the dampened area to soak up the excess lacquer thinner and to force the softened lacquer film into the mesh of the fabric (Fig. 4–32). Do not rub any more than you need. As soon as the film takes on a darker and duller tone, that part has adhered; leave it alone, and go on to the next small area, and the next, until the entire film has an even darker, duller tone indicating that it has all adhered.

After the film and screen have dried for at least twenty minutes, carefully separate the heavy wax paper from the lacquer film at one end with a dull knife. Grasp the wax paper firmly with both hands and slowly peel it off the lacquer (Fig. 4–33). Watch very closely. Occasionally a portion of the lacquer film may not have adhered properly but if caught in time can be loosened carefully with a knife edge. When the wax paper is removed, closely inspect the stencil against the light. If there are loose edges, adhere them by rubbing them quickly and carefully with a small rag slightly dampened with lacquer thinner or adherent. While doing this, place the screen silk on a pad of absorbent newspaper. Small holes or damage can be repaired with a fine brush and clear lacquer. If the lacquer film does not completely cover the fabric of the stencil frame, and there is no need that it should, the open areas of the fabric can be sealed by scraping clear lacquer over them with a small piece of cardboard. When making repairs with lacquer, be sure that the silk fabric is not resting on any surface or it will stick.

Fig. 4–30. The parts of film peeled off make up the design to be printed.

Fig. 4–31. One secret to adhering lacquer film is to work quickly, using a rag heavily saturated with solvent.

Fig. 4–32. Excess solvent must be picked up quickly with a dry cloth and a minimum of rubbing.

Fig. 4–33. Care must be used in peeling the wax paper off the dried lacquer film.

Fig. 4–34. Plastic gloves are a good protection against lacquer solvent, which is used to remove lacquer film from the screen.

Fig. 4–35. Textures and color shading can be reproduced with a lithographic crayon.

Fig. 4–36. Lithographic tusche is applied with a brush to those areas that are to print solid.

Fig. 4–37. The screen should be held at a sharp angle while the glue mixture is being applied.

In the same manner you printed the other three colors, print the fourth color on each paper in your edition. When finished, clean the frame thoroughly again. After the paint is cleaned from the printing frame, the lacquer film can be taken off the fabric with a rag soaked in lacquer thinner (Fig. 4–34). Apply the lacquer thinner liberally on both sides of the screen and place the fabric on a pad of old newspapers. This will soak up a good deal of the old lacquer. If you used clear lacquer to protect the tapes on your printing frame, you will now have to re-paint the frame with clear lacquer to keep it protected. If you used clear shellac, the lacquer thinner will *not* dissolve it.

Color five—a glue and lithographic tusche stencil. Lay the screen mesh over the original sketch and indicate or trace with pencil those areas on which you want to use the lithographic crayon. Then, if you want a rough texture or a shaded color, place the screen mesh on the back, textured surface of a piece of Masonite (other textured surfaces can be used). Crayon in the indicated areas with a soft greasy lithographic crayon. Press quite hard. If you

look at Fig. 4–35 closely, you will see the texture of the Masonite back repeated in the crayon texture on the screen. Then, using liquid lithographic tusche and a brush, paint heavier solid areas and lines on the screen (Fig. 4–36).

Mix a solution of 40 per cent hide glue (similar to Le-Page's), 50 per cent water, 8 per cent white vinegar, and 2 per cent glycerin. Hold one end of the frame up at a rather steep angle. Pour a quantity of this glue and water mixture at the lower edge inside the screen. With a stiff piece of cardboard wide enough to cover your stencil, scrape the solution quickly and smoothly up to the top of the inside of the screen (Fig. 4–37). Turn the cardboard scraper around and quickly scrape the excess back down to the lower edge of the inside of the frame. Drain off the excess into the mixing jar and allow the screen to dry. The glue does not adhere to the tusche or crayon. Repeat the gluing step to fill up the small air bubbles left after the first coating and to give you a glue coat that will hold up better in the printing process. Allow the second glue coat to dry.

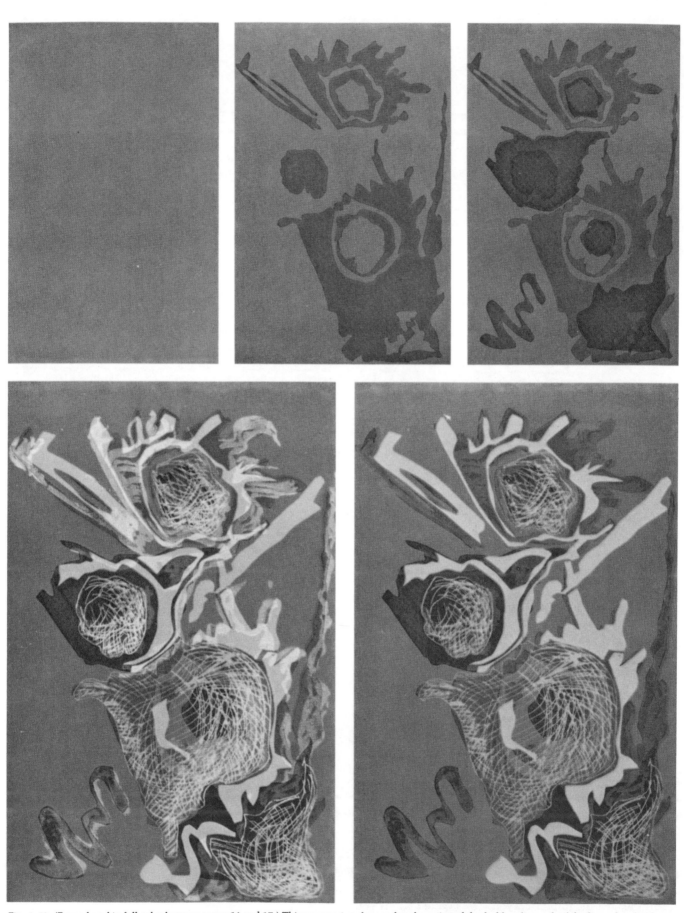

Fig. 4–41. (Reproduced in full color between pages 16 and 17.) This progression shows what the serigraph looks like after each of the five colors has been added.

Fig. 4–40. The fifth color is being printed with the tusche and glue resist.

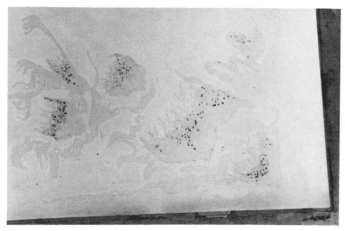

Fig. 4–38. Paint thinner or turpentine is used to clean the crayon and tusche from the screen.

Fig. 4–39. The screen is ready for printing. Small black dots of crayon and tusche remain, which is desirable for the print being made, but these can be removed by more careful cleaning if you wish.

When the second glue coat has dried, place the screen on old newspapers with the underside up. Using a rag and paint thinner or turpentine, loosen and remove as much of the lithographic crayon and tusche as you can (Fig. 4–38). Turn the screen over on the newspapers and continue cleaning. Repeat this process working first on one side and then the other until as much of the lithographic crayon and tusche is removed as suits your purposes. You can get it all out by holding the screen upright and scrubbing it with soaked rags simultaneously on both sides. In Fig. 4–39 a bit of the crayon and tusche (the black spots) was left in to break up the somewhat regular texture of the back of the Masonite.

Now you can print the fifth color (Fig. 4–40).

5. MAKING A FABRIC PRINT

The Textile Printing Frame and Printing Board

Textile printing frames are constructed in exactly the same manner as are the frames used for serigraphs. Even the cardboard box with organdy described in Chapter 3 can be used by a child for simple textile printing. The difference between the two processes is primarily the way in which the printing frame is used. While the serigraphic printing frame is stationary and hinged on a flat board, the textile printing frame is moved along a long padded board as each unit of the design is printed, guided by gauge bolts on a key rail.

The *printing board* (Fig. 5–2) is constructed with a piece of Masonite nailed and supported on an under-framing of 1- by 2-inch clear pine lumber; then it is padded and covered. Cotton flannel sheets or flannel summer blankets provide good padding as long as you use a double thickness. Cut to size and stretch a double layer of cloth over the surface of the board and staple it at the edges. Cover the padding with vinyl or oilcloth of a dark color, preferably black, stretching it very tightly and smoothly and stapling it down at the outside edges.

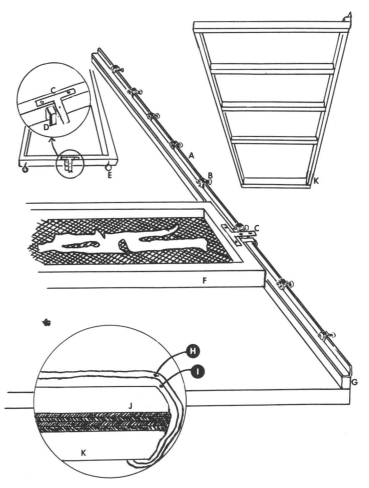

Fig. 5–1. Textile designer Patricia Mansfield gets ready to print a piece of fabric. Some of her finished fabric designs are hung on the wall behind her and on the drying rack at right.

Fig. 5–2. The diagram shows the basic construction of a textile printing board. The frame in the upper right-hand corner is a firm supporting base of 1-by-2-inch lumber for the board. The basic parts of the board are: key rail (*A*); key bolts (*B*); T bar (*C*); J bar (*D*); screw eyes (*E*); printing frame (*F*); 1-by-2-inch lumber that raises the key rail to the proper height (*G*); surface covering of oilcloth or plastic, preferably black or a dark color (*H*); padding made of felt or flannel sheeting (*I*); Masonite board (*J*); 1-by-2-inch support for the Masonite (*K*).

The spacing on the key rail is adjusted by pouncing some powdered chalk through the screen, and a dark background color is needed so that the chalk print can be seen (Fig. 5–3).

Since Masonite is sold in 4-foot widths, printing boards are usually 24 or 48 inches wide. They should be at least 5 or 6 feet long. The narrower board is portable and convenient to store and use, particularly for people in small apartments. It is adequate for printing small pieces of fabric and short pattern runs. However, many more repositionings of both the screen and the fabric are needed if longer or wider textiles are to be printed. The wider board allows you to print the full width of most fabrics without repositioning. The longer the board, the longer the piece of textile that can be printed with one positioning. Professional textile printing tables are often 100 to 200 feet long. The board should not be wider than 48

Fig. 5–3. A chalked test print for keying the gauge bolts shows up on the dark printing board. The fabric at right has been partially printed.

inches because the printer must be able to reach easily past the middle of the board. If a screen covers the full width of the printing board, then two printers are necessary, one on each side to pass the squeegee between them.

A metal angle iron (¾ by ¾ inches) must be screwed along the entire length of one side of a 24-inch printing board and along both long sides of a 48-inch board to serve as a key rail. Ideally, the key rail should be as high as the side of the printing frame. The rail may need to be elevated on a small piece of wood nailed to the printing board for higher printing frames.

The interior dimensions of the *wooden printing frame* should be at least 3 inches wider and 6 inches longer than the size of the largest design unit you expect to print. Each printing frame should have a metal T plate screwed at the center of one end (Fig. 5–4) to act as a contact point with the gauge bolt on the key rail.

To hold the frame firmly against the key rail, a metal J bar is fastened on the edge of the printing frame next to the T plate (Fig. 5–5). You will not be able to purchase such a bar, but one can be bent easily in a vise with a hammer. Buy an ordinary small flat metal reinforcing bar along with the T plate. Near each end of the side of the printing frame holding the T plate, drill a small hole (to prevent the wood from cracking) and screw in two fairly large screw eyes. These will be screwed in and out to keep the printed units parallel with each other. The screw eyes rest against the key rail in the printing process. Gauge bolts set in place along the key rail allow the screen to be placed at accurate intervals when a continuous run is being printed. They are easily adjusted by a turn of the screw. Gauge bolts (called stair gauges and usually sold in pairs), T plates, screw eyes, and the flat metal bar used in making the J bar are available in hardware stores.

Fig. 5–4. A closeup look at the printing frame clearly shows the arrangement of the T plate (A), J bar (B), screw eye (C), key rail and gauge bolt (D).

Fig. 5–5. During printing, the J bar (immediately to the right of the T bar) holds the frame in place against the key rail.

Preparing a Stencil Using a
Light-Sensitive Gelatin Emulsion

All methods for producing a stencil resist that we have discussed so far can be used in screen-printing textiles. Just follow the directions given. Now we will discuss the production of a light-sensitive gelatin stencil and show you some of its uses in textile printing. This process can also be used in the printing of serigraphs. Nylon screens must be used with this emulsion.

There are three means of preventing the light from reaching portions of a sensitized emulsion in order to produce a stencil. First, there are actual objects and materials. These could be cord, bits of metal or wire, or other objects picked up where you happen to be (Fig. 5–6). They are placed directly on the screen, and their opacity blocks out the light reaching the emulsion. The second method is to use a sheet of acetate upon which designs have been painted with black opaque paint. Even press-type letters can be adhered to the acetate. The third is a photographic negative or positive taken with a camera. Many ordinary negatives do not have enough contrast and have to be printed or enlarged on an orthochromatic high-contrast film like Kodalith, which gives very interesting effects. However, if you want to retain a halftone effect, a halftone screen will have to be used in exposing the Kodalith.

The first thing you must do is carefully prepare the solution sensitizer and the gelatin emulsion. Future difficulties will be avoided if you keep all pans and containers clean and carefully follow all directions.

Solution sensitizer. Mix 1 tablespoon of ammonium bichromate (available from a screen-process supply house) in ½ cup of cool water. Wear rubber or plastic gloves: the solution is quite toxic. It will keep for several months, if carefully sealed, in a dark cabinet in a dark bottle. Since only 2 tablespoons are used each time, the above quantity will produce a number of stencils. Keep this solution cool: preferably never above 60 degrees.

Gelatin emulsion. This will make enough emulsion to cover one large screen (about 20 by 30 inches) with three coats. Since the emulsion will not keep, mix it up as needed. It must be used in a darkened room.

Heat 1 cup of water, but not above 167 degrees. It is very likely that the water coming from your hot-water tap will be hot enough. While preparing and using the emulsion, keep it hot by setting the mixing can in a larger container of hot tap water. Add 1 teaspoon of Keltex. Beat the mixture with an egg beater after adding each of the ingredients to ensure that the emulsion will remain smooth. Add a scant ½ teaspoon of Calgon (sodium hexametaphosphate). Next add ½ teaspoon of dark fabric dye (purple, green, or blue) to make it easier to see the stencil on the printing screen. Then add 2 tablespoons of ordinary granulated household gelatin.

You must now darken the room, although it does not have to be completely dark. The light from a 25-watt yellow insect lamp can be used for illumination. The emulsion is then made light-sensitive by adding 2 tablespoons of the liquid ammonium-bichromate sensitizer mixed earlier. Beat it with an egg beater.

If you are not going to use the screens right away, you may find it more convenient to apply the unsensitized emulsion to the screen fabric. The screen can then be stored for an indefinite period. When you wish to use the screen, coat it with the sensitized emulsion on both sides. This must be done very evenly so that the emulsion does not wash off the previous coat (which is water soluble before being exposed to the light). A wide brush can be used with a light, quick touch. A scooper coater (available from screen-process supply houses) can also be used. The screen can be sensitized in a light room, but avoid direct sunlight or intense light. The screen will not be fully light sensitive until the emulsion has dried. Dry the sensitized screen in a flat position. A vertical or slanted position will cause certain portions of the emulsion to dissolve with the flow of the sensitizer.

A sensitized emulsion must be applied to the screen fabric in the darkened room. (Again use the insect bulb for illumination. The unsensitized emulsion does not require a dark room during application.)

Fig. 5–6. Even the bottom of a wire basket can create an interesting design pattern for a light-sensitive emulsion resist.

Fig. 5–7. Coating the screen with a light-sensitive photo emulsion is easy with this specially constructed scooper coater, but a stiff piece of cardboard can also be used.

Fig. 5–8. A spiral of black yarn laid out on the light-sensitive emulsion and held down flat with a heavy piece of plate glass is now being exposed to the light.

Prop the screen up at a sharp angle and place the bottom of the frame on old newspapers or in a tray to catch overflow (see Fig. 5–7). Pour some of the prepared emulsion in a scooper coater. Tilt the scooper and quickly pull it upward over the screen, coating the entire surface. Turn the screen around and repeat the procedure on its other side. Any excess emulsion that has gathered around the edges can be wiped away with soft cleansing tissues. Do not touch the screen area with the tissues. Allow the frame to dry. The drying must take place in the darkened room or storage space if the emulsion has been sensitized. The drying may be speeded up with an electric fan or hair dryer.

After drying the first coat, repeat the process with a second coat on each side of the screen. If the first two coats are thin, you may need a third coat on each side.

While the scooper coater is an inexpensive, labor-saving device, it is not absolutely essential. You can coat the screen by placing it flat on a table propped up so that the screen mesh does not touch the table. Pour a little emulsion in one end of the frame and carefully scrape it across the screen with a cardboard until the screen is coated evenly. Turn the screen over and repeat on the other side. Allow this to dry (in the darkened room if your emulsion is sensitized) and when dry, repeat the process.

After the screen has dried, arrange resist materials (in Fig. 5–8, a coiled piece of heavy black yarn is used) on the surface of the sensitized screen. Hold it in place with a heavy sheet of plate glass. A sheet of black paper placed under the screen prevents the light from bouncing up on the gelatin and exposing it in the wrong areas. Expose the screen to a No. 2 photoflood lamp hung about 3 feet from the emulsion surface. You will have to experiment with your material to find the correct exposure time, but you might begin with an exposure of 30 minutes. When the light is turned off, uncover the screen.

If the emulsion has been properly exposed, you will see a faint brown image on it. Move the screen to the sink and wash or spray it carefully with lukewarm water (90 to 115 degrees). A rubber shower spray is inexpensive and can be attached to most faucets. Wash or spray the warm water on both sides of the screen. Avoid a hard spray, which will damage the soft gelatin. If the screen is properly exposed, the areas protected from the light by the resist materials will wash away, leaving clear areas to form the stencil. If the entire image washes away, one of three things could be wrong: the exposure has not been long enough; the water is too hot; the spray has too much pressure. If the image does not wash out, one of two things could be wrong: the water is not warm enough; the exposure has been too long. When the stencil has been washed clean, rinse it with cold water to harden the gelatin and set it aside to dry.

Fig. 5–9. The unexposed part of the emulsion on the screen washes out and the spiral pattern of the yarn becomes evident. It is being overprinted on another pattern already on the fabric.

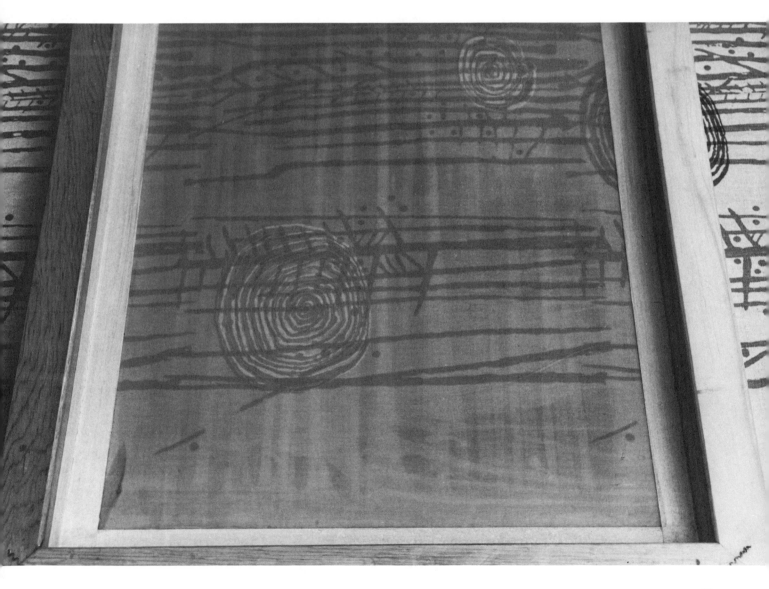

When dry, the stencil should be checked for pinholes or damage. If you saved the emulsion that you had left over, use it with a small brush for patching areas and holes in the screen. If it is too thick, warm it by setting it in a pan of hot water. It can be applied in ordinary light since you want it to harden anyhow. When the stencil has dried, it is ready for printing.

If you do not wish to make your own emulsion, excellent ones are available from the screen-process supply companies. If you follow the manufacturer's directions for sensitizing the emulsions, quantities as small as one ounce can be mixed. The sensitized emulsions will keep for a period of several weeks if stored in a cool, dry place.

Fig. 5–10. Tops cut from cleansing tissue boxes form a pattern to be exposed on a light-sensitive emulsion. The final design printed on corduroy is made more interesting with a buglike form printed in a second color with a second stencil.

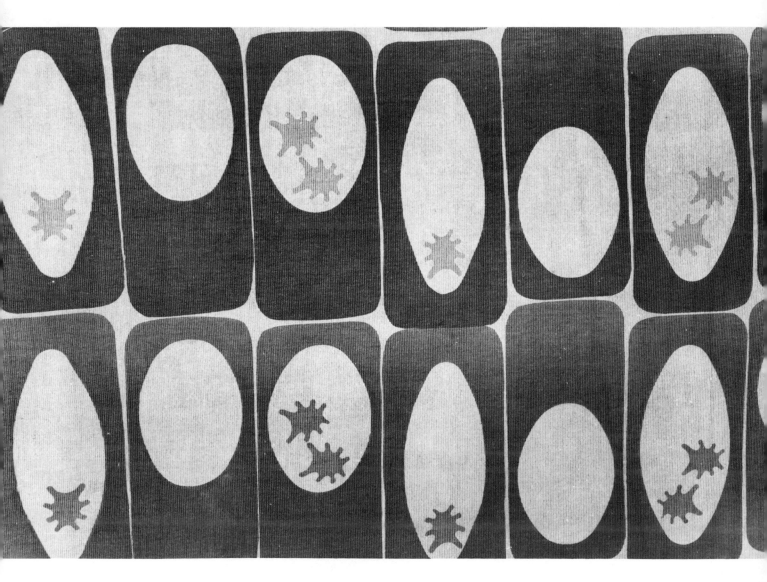

Fig. 5–11. Folded cut paper is basic to this design for a light-sensitive gelatin-emulsion resist, which is shown printed in a number of ways. The textured section was made on another screen by exposing a remnant of fabric with many threads pulled out. (By Carole Bansemer)

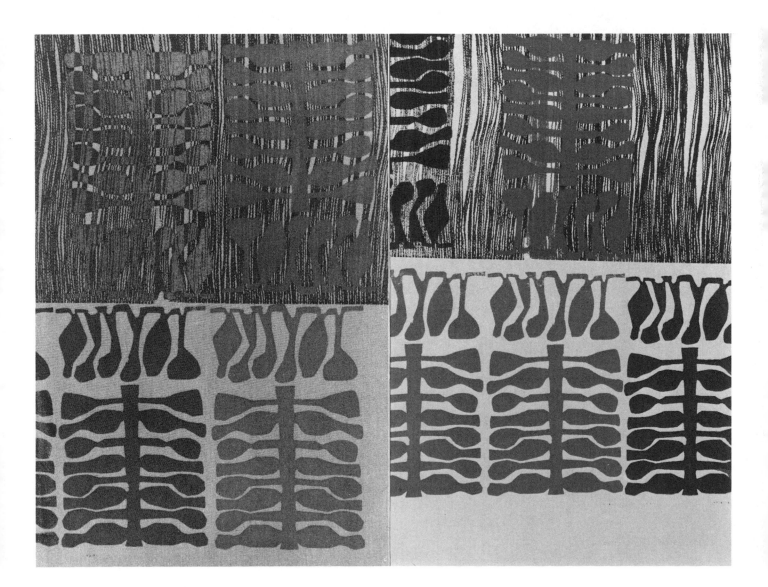

Using a Presensitized Commercial Photo-Stencil Film to Print Textiles

There are a number of presensitized gelatin films that can be used in place of the gelatin-emulsion stencil just described. They are all easier to use, but they are considerably more expensive. Each of the films has different characteristics as to film speed, permanency, kind of detail resolution, and development. Choose the type best suited for your purpose and then follow the manufacturer's directions carefully.

First, mix the chemical or chemicals used in the developing process. Then paint the design in black on an acetate sheet (Fig. 5–12). Expose it to light with the sensi-

tized film, develop the film, then wash out the unexposed parts of the film and adhere it to the screen according to the manufacturer's directions. Nylon screen must be used for *some* light-sensitive films; others can be used on silk. Check the directions before choosing your screen mesh. After the film stencil has been adhered to the frame and dried, check it for pinholes. These holes and any open parts of the screen around the outside edge of the stencil are blocked out with lacquer. All types of stencils can be repaired or blocked out with lacquer.

Fig. 5–12.   A design is painted on a piece of clear acetate (right), which is then placed on a presensitized emulsion film, exposed to light, developed, and adhered to the screen (left) ready for printing.

Fig. 5–13. (Reproduced in full color between pages 16 and 17.) Two strikingly different effects are achieved in basically the same way. Seed pods, dried stalks of grain, and cut paper were used to make the designs on light-sensitive resists, and overlapping in the printing process built up the pattern sequences. (Top, by Barbara C. Knollenberg; bottom, by Patricia Zuzinec)

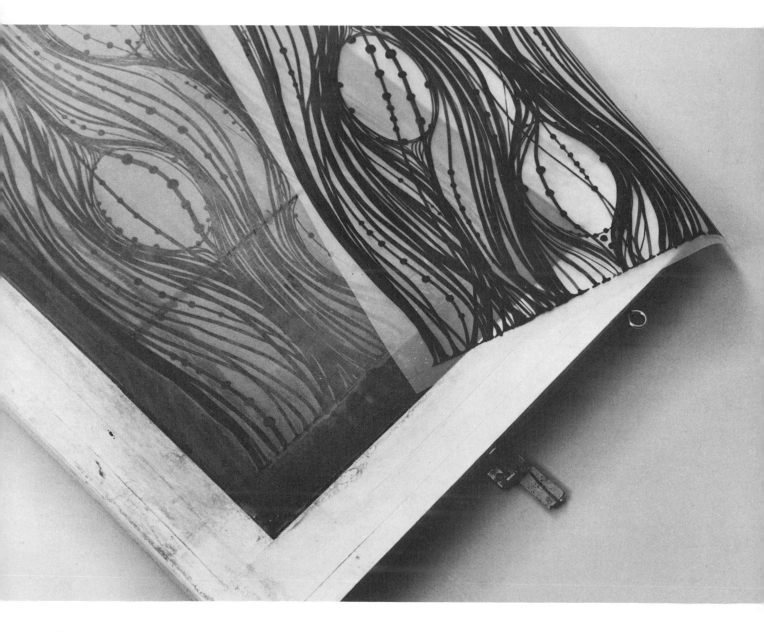

Fig. 5–14. The placement of the frame for printing the design is tested by rubbing white carpenter's chalk through the screen onto the surface of the printing board.

Fig. 5–15. Positioning of the gauge bolt on the key rail so that the screen will properly print the second unit of the design is also experimental and must be tested with chalk.

Fig. 5–16. After the first two gauge bolts have been properly positioned, the distance between them is measured and set on a gauge stick.

The easiest way to experiment with placement and adjustments in spacing a textile pattern is with chalk (Fig. 5–14). Place the dried screen as close to the end of the printing board as possible and fasten a stair gauge to the key rail snug against the left edge of the T plate. Let the screw eyes rest firmly against the key rail. The three points of contact will automatically assure a consistent placement of the stencil when a repeat pattern is desired. Lightly rub or pounce chalk powder through the stencil openings onto the dark printing board. (If powdered chalk is not available at your hardware or paint store, powdered tempera paint will work, but it is not as finely ground and does not give as clear an image.)

Lift the stencil frame, check the chalked image, and then experiment with the placement of a second image. Trial areas can be chalked and erased to see how the design will fit together—whether it should overlap, interlock, or have a space between. When the final placement of the image has been determined, fasten a second stair gauge to the key rail (Fig. 5–15). Again place it snug against the left side of the T plate. A gauge stick can be improvised by slipping a pair of gauge bolts onto an ordinary yardstick or a strip of thin lumber and matching the distance between them to the distance between the two bolts attached to the key rail on the printing board (Fig. 5–16). This gauge stick will allow you to place the rest of the gauges along the length of the key rail to give the precise points for setting your screen down for each pattern unit (Fig. 5–17). When the pattern has been chalked lightly along the whole length of the printing board (Fig. 5–18), use strips of masking tape to indicate the location of the print for placing the cloth (Fig. 5–19). The chalk must be brushed and pounded out of the frame. Be certain to wipe out all chalk dust (but do not moisten) before adding printing paint.

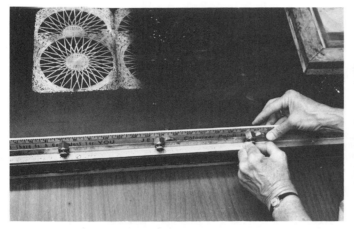

Fig. 5–17. Using the gauge stick makes easy work of setting the remaining gauge bolts along the key rail.

Fig. 5–18. When all of the gauge bolts are placed, it is a good idea to test the accuracy of the alignment of the design along the entire length of the printing board with chalk.

Fig. 5–19. A band of masking tape along the beginning edge and one side of the chalk design will help in positioning the fabric for printing. Before placing the fabric, remove the chalk on the board with a dry rag.

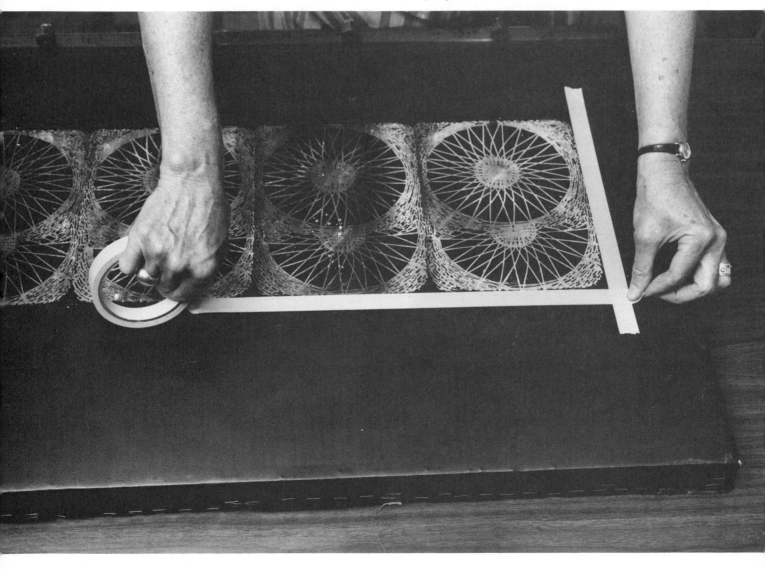

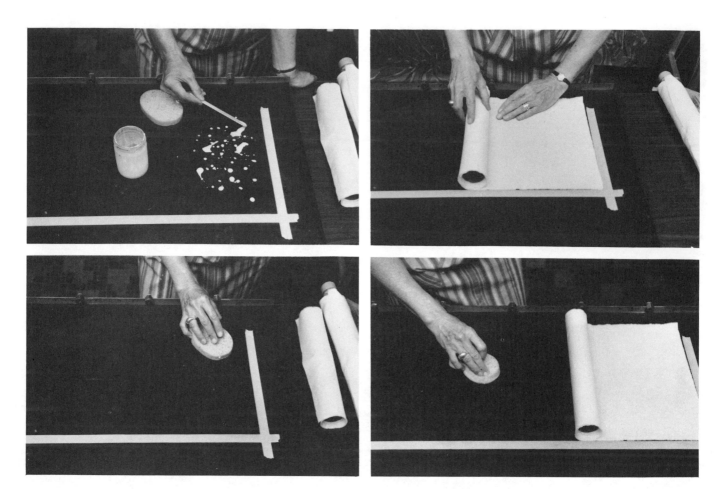

Fig. 5–20.   To hold the fabric in place, a small amount of casein glue thinned with water is dribbled on the board.

Fig. 5–21.   A damp sponge spreads the glue evenly and thinly on the surface. Since the glue dries rapidly, only a small area of the board should be done before you start laying out the fabric. The surface of the board should be slightly tacky.

Fig. 5–22.   The fabric must be very carefully rolled smoothly and evenly onto the area of the board just covered with glue.

Fig. 5–23.   Alternate gluing the board and unrolling the fabric until the length of fabric to be printed is laid out.

The fabric to be printed should now be placed in position and its distance from the edge of the key rail measured. If the pattern is not a very complicated one, or if it is to be printed in no more than one color, or if the cloth is very firm and heavy, the fabric to be printed can simply be taped to the printing board with masking tape. However, to ensure a register accurate enough for multicolor designs, complicated patterns, and sheer fabric, the cloth should be lightly glued to the surface of the board. Mix one part white casein glue to one part water until the water becomes slightly sticky between the fingers.

Have your roll of fabric ready. Starting at one end of the printing board, sprinkle a few drops of this glue-and-water solution over the surface (Fig. 5–20). With a damp sponge, spread the solution over the board's width for 12 or 15 inches, until the surface is slightly sticky to the touch (Fig. 5–21). Standing glue must be sponged up or it may color the cloth. Should you inadvertently get a little too much glue somewhere on the fabric and a spot develops, do not worry about it; it will probably disappear when it dries, but try to avoid this. Unroll about 12

to 15 inches of the fabric. Lay it in position on the printing board (Fig. 5–22) and press it firmly, smoothly, and carefully onto the section of board on which you have just spread the glue. Continue until the entire fabric has been adhered (Fig. 5–23). Keep the edges of the cloth parallel to the edges of the printing board as you go. With skill, you will be able to glue sheer silk to the printing board with little or none of the glue showing.

You are now ready for the printing. Textile dye or paint is placed in one end of the frame, and (if yours is a full-width 48-inch board) the squeegee is pushed across the board and rhythmically and smoothly passed over to a second printer on the other side (Fig. 5–24). This takes a little practice but can be learned fairly easily. Contrary to the printing of serigraphs, where the squeegee is pulled over each paper only once, the squeegee in textile painting may have to be pulled back and forth as many as four

Fig. 5–24. Having two printers to pass the squeegee back and forth from one side of the board to the other is virtually a necessity if you are printing on a full-width board.

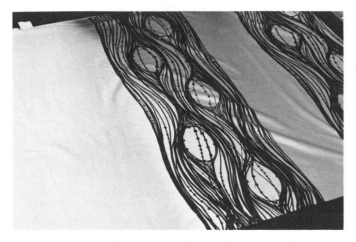

Fig. 5–25. Backprinting is avoided by printing every other unit along the length of the board first.

Fig. 5–26. If the first units are not yet dry when the intervening units are printed, cover them with clean newsprint so that you do not pick up any of the design from them and transfer it with the screen.

Fig. 5–27. Each unit of the final print used previously as an example is partially overlapped, and the designer has alternated red and black design units. This gives an interesting overlay effect in the transparent colors.

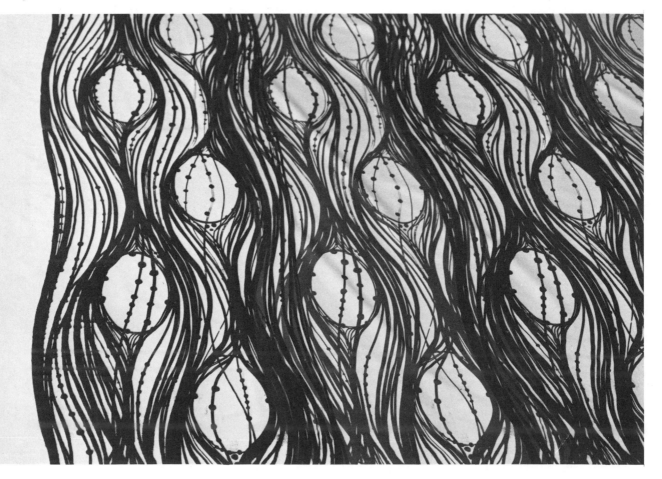

Fig. 5–28. With a small apartment-sized printing board it is possible for one person to do the printing job without assistance.

or five times in each direction. Fabric is much more absorbent than printing paper, and more dye or paint must be forced into the fibers. The thicker, coarser, more absorbent fabrics like homespun require more pulls of the squeegee. On very sheer fabrics such as silk one pull may be adequate. Ordinary percale requires three passes of the squeegee in each direction. Only printing experience with many different fabrics will give you the skill and knowledge you need for this.

It is wise to print alternate design units (Figs. 5–25 and 5–26): units one, three, five, for example, should be printed first; then return to print units two, four, and six.

In long runs, the paint of the first run is dry before the second run is started. In short runs, the printed image will still be wet, so sheets of newspaper cut to the size of the design unit should be readily available. Cover the wet units with this newspaper when printing adjacent to them to avoid "backprinting." A backprint is the result of ink picked up on the underside of the screen leaving an undesired print when the screen is laid down the next time. These unwanted images can be avoided by using newspaper or by wiping the wet ink from the underside of the screen each time.

Fig. 5–29. Each recently printed design unit should be protected with clean newsprint while the unit next to it is being printed.

If you wish to print a short piece of fabric on a half-width board (2 by 6 feet), first tape the cloth in the proper position. One hand keeps the frame from slipping while the other operates the squeegee. If you are printing a long piece, have an assistant hold the screen firmly in place, freeing you to use both hands with full consistent pressure on the squeegee stroke. On short boards the pattern units must be printed in succession and the cloth shifted along as you go. Remember to protect a wet unit with newsprint while the next one is being printed (Fig. 5–29), then pick it up so that drying of the design is not impeded.

Fig. 5–30.   A textile designer evaluates a print she has just completed.

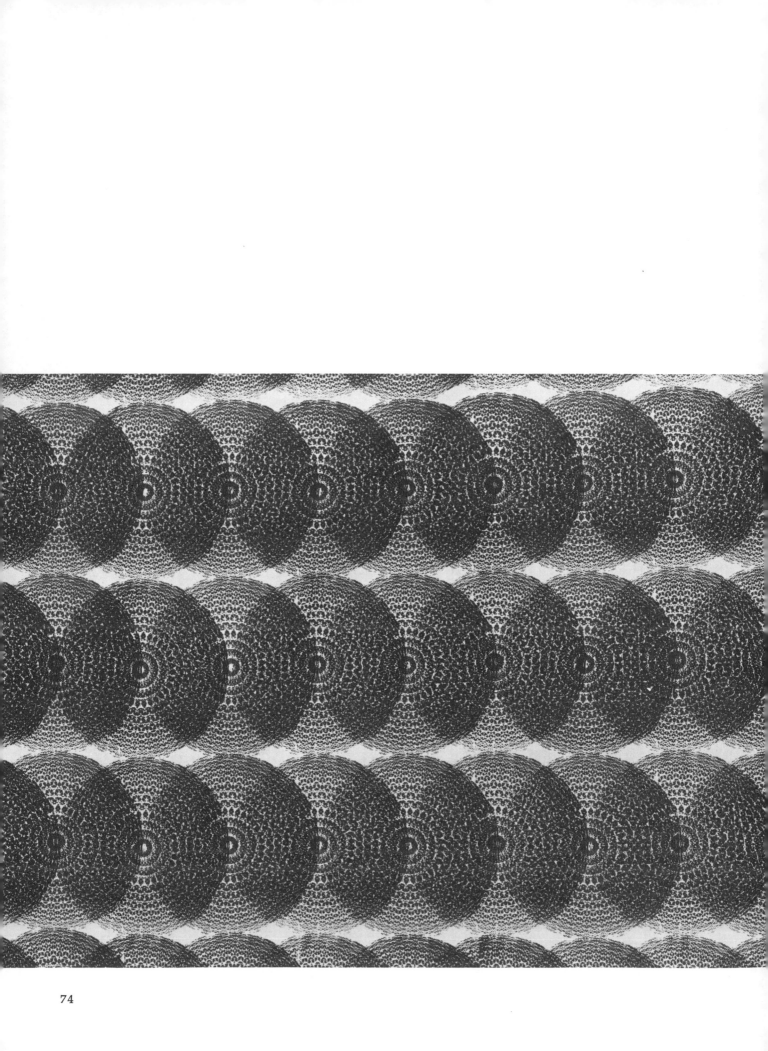

74

6. POSSIBILITIES WITH RESISTS

We are going to shift our approach somewhat in the hope that it will give you a broad understanding of the process as well as reinforce and further elaborate on what we have already said. The preceding chapters give an idea of the complete screen process. However, this process is very flexible and contains many variations, and we would like to discuss some of them in detail in the next several chapters. Unavoidably, there will be a little repetition, but it will help to jell the ideas already in your mind.

The major problem of a how-to-do-it book, as this professes to be, is that interest in the problems of technique and physical manipulation of the medium are given so much space and importance. One is apt to forget that technical craftsmanship and skill are completely subordinate to the idea presented, the artist's conception. This is the only reason for making the print or producing the textile in the first place. The technique must never stand in the way of the idea's clarity and potency or the result will be merely a brilliant show of technical virtuosity. Technique with no purpose is impressive but useless.

Yet craftsmanship and technical competence are important, particularly to the beginner. And, in a manner, this must come first. With experience, it is hoped that techniques will become intuitive. Then the major effort of the artist and designer can be directed at the idea that he is expressing in his textile design or serigraphic print.

Fig. 6–1. A presensitized screen-process film was used to make the stencil for this textile print. ("Circles," by Patricia K. Mansfield)

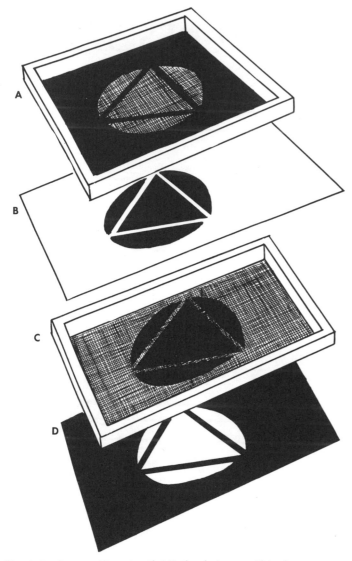

Fig. 6-2. In a positive stencil (A) the design motif is the open area that lets ink pass through to print the design on paper or fabric (B). In a negative stencil (C) only the background area is open for ink to pass through. On the print made with the negative stencil (D) the design motif is the only part not covered with ink.

The stencil is a resist that prevents the paint or ink from reaching parts of the printed image. Basically there are two types of stencils, positive and negative (Fig. 6-2). In the positive stencil, the resist material fills in the background, and the actual image is printed. This is the normal way of looking at objects, and therefore positive stencils are a little easier to work with. Paper stencils, cut films, washout-resist stencils, and most photographic stencils are positive images. In the negative stencil, the resist material is applied to the screen as an actual image. Most direct blockout stencils and some photographic stencils are negative-image processes.

It has been claimed that there are over forty-five different kinds of stencils prepared for the commercial screen-process industry alone, and individual serigraphic artists and textile designers have added considerably to that enormous proliferation of resist methods.

Unfortunately, the process itself is so intriguing that one becomes fascinated with new ways of making a resist. Actually, an artist should use no more stencils or different kinds of stencils than serve the clarity and strength of his final visual statement. Some printers use too many stencils. You can produce an excellent print or fabric design using only one stencil, and most prints and designs do not require more than three or four stencils to make complex and effective images. So discipline yourself and select your stencils sparingly and carefully. On the other hand, there is no reason to limit the number of stencils used if your statement would be more effective with additional ones. For example, certain rich, lustrous transparent colors may need a rather large build-up of different stencils before the desired effect is achieved.

For any multistencil design, four register marks should be drawn on each screen at the very beginning of the designing process, and they should then be included on every stencil no matter how produced. This assures accurate placement of each stencil resist on the printing frame (Figs. 6-3 and 6-4). In printing a serigraph it is also helpful to print the register marks on each print run in the margin of the print. This gives one more helpful check on the accuracy of the register of each color. The marks can be trimmed off the print or covered by the mat in mounting.

One other caution can be applied generally to all stencil production: the screen fabric stretched on the frame that will serve as the support for your stencil resist must be scrupulously clean. See Chapter 8 for procedures.

Fig. 6-3. The four black crosses on the stencil are register marks.

Fig. 6-4. The register marks should be printed on the first trial proofs prints of an edition to check accuracy and then be blocked out on the screen for the running of the actual edition. If the register marks are on the margin of a print, they can be left on during the run and later trimmed off or covered with a mat.

Fig. 6–5. The large free-form shapes in this serigraph were printed with paper stencils. (By Russell Peterson)

The Paper Stencil

The use of paper for the stencil resist is a simple, economical, and fast way to produce a screen print. The paper stencil is an excellent first experience for the beginner because it is an approach basic to the design process, and it is also easy, flexible and rewarding. Creating cut shapes frees him from some confining design clichés. The cut-paper shape is very different from a shape that is drawn. The shapes can be cut and used simply as a design exercise, without printing or adhering them to the screen fabric. The stencils can be cut and arranged in many trial ways. The positive forms (the parts cut out), because they are cut out of the paper, are visually sympathetic to it. They can be combined easily in a variety of ways. They can even be adhered as a stencil on the screen for a resist and printed. Many artists like to use paper stencils in the experimental first stages of a print. Or they can be used as a basis for a cut-film stencil if you place transparent film over the shapes and cut it. In the photo-stencil process, if the cutouts are opaque enough, they can serve to block out the light in exposure.

Almost any paper can be used for paper stencils, depending on what effect you have in mind. The paper used is usually transparent—or can be made transparent—and will not allow the paint to seep through it. It will stand up under a short run. Most paper stencils will give fifty to a hundred good clear impressions. Opaque paper can be used if you are designing the print directly with the paper stencil shapes and not working with a preliminary sketch. Ordinary blank newsprint makes an economical and satisfactory stencil, but it will wear out sooner than stronger papers.

Thin papers and very absorbent papers, like some tissue papers and rice paper, may allow the paint or ink to seep through during the printing process. Normally this is to be avoided, but for special effects and for short runs it can be controlled. A number of trial prints must be made first until the seepage is stabilized at the level you need. Then you must use a fairly light, consistent squeegee pressure. Check each print to see that the seepage does not become excessive. When it does, replace the paper stencil with a second paper stencil, cut simultaneously with the first one so that it is an exact duplicate. In this manner, normal print consistency is possible and special textural effects can be achieved.

Ordinary household freezer wrapping paper with a plastic coating can be used. The first pass of the printing ink with the squeegee will adhere the paper to the screen meshes if it is lightly fastened to the underside of the frame with masking tape before hard. This is reasonably durable even with water-soluable inks.

The common stencil paper used by house painters should not be used for most prints because it is thick and will deposit a heavy coating of paint on the print. On the other hand, if you want an impasto effect, you can get it by using just such a thick, or even thicker, paper stencil, for the layer of ink deposited will be just as thick as the stencil used. Paper stencils, even the thinner ones, deposit more ink than most other stencil-resist methods.

Waxy papers are generally not satisfactory for paper resists, because they tend to repel paints, especially water-based paints.

Papers that are not naturally transparent can be made transparent by rubbing them with a rag soaked in mineral spirits, cooking oil, or kerosene. They should then be pressed for a while between layers of paper towels to soak out the excess oil.

Weaker papers like newsprint and some of the tissue papers can be made stronger by coating them or, better still, spraying them with four coats of shellac or clear lacquer; this will also make them transparent. Papers that have been so treated will adhere more firmly to the stencil fabric. If you have used shellac, place the paper under the frame, shellacked side up against the mesh, with absorbent paper (several thicknesses of paper towels or a desk blotter will do) over the silk on the inside of the frame. Then apply heat with a warm iron on the absorbent paper inside the frame, checking frequently to see if the paper has adhered. All you need to do is heat the paper sufficiently to soften the shellac. Lacquered paper can be applied like a lacquer-film stencil (see page 89).

Clear thin acetate can also be used effectively in this manner. The acetate is given four coats of shellac, cut, and then ironed onto the screen the same way shellacked paper is. A minimum amount of heat should be used.

When you cut a stencil, it is important to use a very sharp knife and to keep it sharp by rubbing it on a finely ground oil stone as you work. The cutting surface must be hard and very smooth. Glass has many advantages. It has a hard, firm surface, although the knife must be sharpened more frequently. In addition, it can be placed right over the sketch and will protect the sketch during cutting. If the stencil paper is not transparent enough for you to follow the sketch easily, it then can be put on a light table or held up to a window. If you need several identical stencils, you can make them accurately by taping together several sheets and cutting them simultaneously. If you are cutting opaque paper or using the stencil as a means of designing, you can use scissors because you are not working over a preplanned sketch.

Many things can be done with paper; only your own imagination will limit you. Instead of cutting the paper, you can tear it into the shapes and holes desired and get softer edges. The edges can be burned with a wood-burning tool, or sandpapered, or the surface of the paper can be roughened with sandpaper to allow some ink to come through it. Holes can be punched with a rotary serrating, or pattern-tracing, wheel creating a dotted-line effect. This wheel can also be used in a step preliminary to tearing out the shape along the serrated line. Holes can be punched in the paper with a paper punch or a leather punch or in any other manner.

Fig. 6–6. If a paper stencil has floating parts it is a good idea to leave the cutout sections in the stencil until it has been adhered to the screen and then pick off the unwanted sections with tweezers. This makes for accurate, easy placement of the floating parts.

The main problems in adhering a paper stencil to the screen mesh are caused by floating parts, thin, delicate peninsulas of paper, and the fragility of most paper stencils. It is the tackiness of the printing ink that holds most paper stencils to the screen mesh. The cut-paper stencil is laid down in position over the sketch on the printing board for a serigraph. In fabric design, where the use of the paper stencil is more informal, positioning needs to be worked out during the printing process. The floating pieces that are part of the design and fragile parts of the stencil are then lightly glued to the screen mesh. A little drop of water-soluble glue is pressed on the screen mesh with a cotton swab until it contacts the paper stencil underneath. Larger pieces may need several such glue drops. The outside edges of the paper stencil are lightly taped to the outside of the printing frame with short pieces of masking tape.

Many artists leave the cutout pieces in the stencil at this point. After the glue has dried, some ink can be placed in the printing frame and squeegeed across to adhere the stencil to the silk. The cutout parts left in the stencil protect the sketch underneath (Fig. 6–6). They are then picked off with tweezers. However, if it is too difficult or time-consuming to leave those pieces in the stencil, the stencil frame will have to be carefully raised after the glue has dried. The sketch is then removed, and a piece of waste printing paper is put in its place. The stencil is printed to attach it securely to the screen. The paper stencil is then taped around the outside edges to prevent the ink from seeping out, and it is ready for printing (see Chapter 3, Step 23).

Generally speaking, paper stencils (unless they have been protected with shellac or lacquer) are not satisfactory for use with water-based inks. They will buckle on the frame and then leak. In textile design, however, they are helpful when a simple direct shape is needed or when you experiment with trial prints.

Since most paper stencils are adhered with the printing ink, they will peel off from the screen when the frame is cleaned. Those parts attached with glue must be washed off with warm water. Stencils coated with shellac and adhered with a warm iron must be removed with alcohol. Stencils coated and adhered with lacquer are removed with lacquer thinner.

The Blockout Resist Stencil

The blockout resist stencil is also a very easy, fast, and economical way to produce a screen resist. It, along with the paper stencil, is an excellent first method for the beginning screen artist (see Chapter 3, Step 25) and easy enough for a child to manipulate. It is also extremely flexible, and, as you will see, your own ingenuity is the only limiting factor.

The blockout resist is generally used as a negative stencil. It is the image or design shape that is easier to apply by painting or adhering. This means that the

Fig. 6–7. The youngster is tracing his design on the screen with fingernail lacquer to make a resist.

background—the space around the design shapes—or negative area, is left open and free for the passage of the paint. Some artists and designers, however, paint or apply the resist to the background areas, creating a positive stencil, even though this is more difficult.

As with the paper stencil, there are many materials that can be used for a blockout and many ways of applying them. Glue is the most common, and it is mixed as follows: 5 ounces of hide glue (like LePage's—the glue must be soluble in water after it has dried), 4 ounces of water, 1 scant ounce of vinegar, and 10 drops of glycerin. Since it has almost no color and is difficult to see when applied, about ½ teaspoon of showcard or tempera color will give it an adequate tint. The glue mixture can also be thinned considerably with water to develop pinholes, if a textured effect is desired, although this is not normally done. The actual amount of thinning is up to the artist.

Other materials that can be painted on the screen are lacquer (tinted with fingernail polish), shellac (tinted with oil colors), liquid wax emulsions (tinted with wax crayons), stove enamel, asphaltum, and any of the several blockout liquids sold by the commercial screen-process supply houses. Ordinary wax crayon can be rubbed on the screen mesh as a blockout, but this works only for water-based paints and even then only for short runs. Oil-based paints tend to dissolve the wax crayon. Cooking paraffin can also be rubbed on the screen mesh in the hard cake form, but it works better melted. Melting paraffin in an electric stew pan with an automatic temperature control reduces the danger of fire. It is applied hot to the screen mesh by any means you want to use. Lumps of hot wax, if they occur, must be scraped off the screen mesh with a dull knife.

But besides liquids that can be painted and solids that can be rubbed on the stencil, there are various adhesive materials that can make blockout resists. Masking tape can be cut in various ways and adhered to the silk. Press-type letters can be stuck to the screen fabric and printed as is, or sprayed with shellac or lacquer around them and then peeled off when the lacquer dries. Use a pressurized can of lacquer for this. When you take the letters off, you will have a positive image that can be printed. Self-adhesive decal paper will also work. It is available in sheet form and in many standard shapes. The paper can be cut or the shapes selected. The protective backing is removed, and the decal adhered in the proper place to the screen.

There are many different ways of applying liquid blockout materials. Any of them can be applied with an ink roller or brayer, with cut and notched pieces of cardboard, crumpled paper, sponges, fingers, sticks, or cotton swabs. They can in many cases be thinned with the appropriate solvent and put on with bamboo pens, ballpoint pens, and even ruling pens. But be very careful not to cut the silk with ruling pens. They may have to be dulled slightly with emery cloth before they will be safe.

If the glue solution is applied to a damp screen fabric, it will produce softer edges. While glue is being applied to a screen, either damp paper or wax paper can be placed underneath. The damp paper can be lifted away after the glue has been applied to the screen mesh. The wax paper can be removed when the glue is partially dried. Each will produce a different effect. If the screen has been given a light coating of machine oil, it will cause the glue to creep and crawl.

Glue and other liquids can be transferred from another surface and printed on the screen mesh. They can be painted on wax paper, for example. The screen is then carefully lowered onto the wax paper so that it is stuck to the silk. Next, the screen is slowly lifted up, and the wax paper carefully peeled off. With wax paper, the glue may be allowed to dry partially before it is removed. All sorts of objects—pieces of wood, various textures of cloth and cardboard, bolts, screws, cross sections of vegetables, and keys, for example—can be given a light coating of liquid glue and then pressed on the screen mesh.

The liquids can be dribbled, poured, and applied by brush or from spouts of plastic mustard containers. A very soft, almost halftone effect can be achieved by placing various shapes or objects on the surface of the screen mesh. Liquid blockout is then sprayed on the screen mesh around those objects with an artist's airbrush. Pressure spray cans of lacquer will also work. Before you use any particular pressure spray paint, be sure that a suitable solvent is available to take it off the screen when the print is finished.

While the liquid blockout is still wet on the screen mesh, objects of various kinds including your own fingers, cotton swabs, and various absorbent papers can be pressed on the wet blockout to blot up some of the liquid. This will also affect the nature of the pattern.

After the liquids have dried, they can be touched with a drop of the proper solvent, which is then allowed to rest on the surface for a short time. Then the surface is wiped quickly with *one* brush of a dry cloth. Stroking more than once will remove too much. Proper stroking will produce small holes in the resist. Edges of the blocked-out areas can be softened by scrubbing them lightly with a brush and the proper solvent.

The blockout resist is particularly adaptable to reduction printing (Fig. 6–8). In brief, this means that a blockout is applied to portions of the screen, and then it is printed. When the print has dried, more of the same blockout is applied and a second color is printed. Up to five or six reduction color runs can be made for one print, with a little more blockout area being added each time. The thickness of the layers of blockout on the screen will call a halt. To make the process less confusing to the artist, the first blockout solution can be tinted a very light color, say white. Then each successive blockout is tinted a slightly different or darker color. This will facilitate design planning during the production process.

Since the last color is printed on all of the previous colors, very rich effects can be achieved, especially when a number of transparent colors are used. A beginner is likely to get a more unified print in this manner, particularly in color and shape. The use of one stencil to which shapes are continually added, reducing the area printed, tends to unify the print. There are a few precautions to be taken with this method. After each new application of the blockout, double-check for the appearance of pinholes. The wear and tear from printing and cleaning frequently produces new pinholes in the old coating. Great care must be taken in the removal of ink after each printing. It tends to stick to the blockout in tiny crevices and, when covered with a new coating, to make final cleaning much more difficult. Because of the number of successive blockout coatings and color printings involved, a blockout resist should never be left on a screen for too long a period, or the screen may turn out to be too difficult to clean. (See Chapter 8 for instructions for removing blockout resists.)

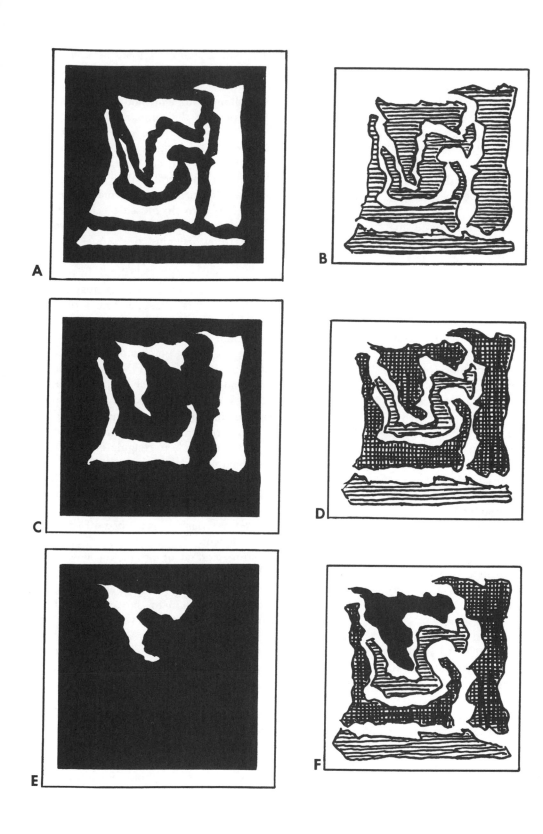

Fig. 6–8. In this drawing, the three stages in making a three-color reduction print are demonstrated. The background area (shown in black) is painted on the screen with lacquer as the resist (A), and the first color is printed (B). Next, the center and lower parts of the design are blocked out on the screen with lacquer (C), and the second color (the cross hatches) is printed over part of the first color (D). Now all of the original design except the top left part is blocked out on the screen with lacquer (E), and the third color is printed (F) over that part of the original design (the black area).

The Washout Resist

The washout resist is the most popular stencil among serigraphers, probably because it is the most autographic stencil and it most resembles the painting process. Its most common form is the well-known tusche-and-glue stencil. In essence, the washout-resist stencil is a double resist method: first, a temporary resist is made, which will be removed from the screen before printing and replaced by a permanent one that will be the printing screen resist.

You will remember that in Chapter 4 we used the common tusche-and-glue resist for one of the color runs. We would like to go over that process again, but in considerably more detail. The repetition may help to make the process clearer. Lithographic tusche in both crayon and liquid form is first applied to those sections of the screen to be printed. To get a cleaner line and more detail, you can first wipe the screen with a cornstarch solution. Mix 2 teaspoons of ordinary cornstarch in a cup of hot water and coat the underside (printing side) of the screen mesh with it. Let it dry before painting the tusche on the screen (Fig. 6–9). It is usually necessary to put two coats of tusche on the screen fabric to get the solid opaque black coating needed. Hold the frame up against a light to check its opacity. In applying the lithographic crayon, press it very hard into the silk in order to fill the meshes. For a textured effect, you can place various materials like corrugated cardboard, pebbled book covers, wall plaster, or wood grain under the screen and then rub the mesh with a lithographic crayon. Again, be sure to get a good deposit of the black crayon on the screen mesh. Liquid tusche can be used to accent these crayon rubbings. When the tusche is dry to the touch or does not rub when touched lightly, it is ready for the glue. It will look shiny and wet: it never gets a completely dry look.

The glue mixture is now scraped with a scraper over the tusche on the inside of the screen (see Chapter 4). An improvement on the cardboard scraper would be one made of tin or aluminum. The scraper should be as wide as the screen area and perfectly straight on the scraping edge. While a metal scraper should have a definite edge, it should not have any nicks or burrs that might damage the screen. The scraping edge should be rubbed down with emery cloth and the ends slightly rounded so that there will be no sharp corners to damage the screen. If you wish, you can place the scraper between two thin slats of wood to form a handle. Metal will scrape cleaner than cardboard, leaving less glue deposited on the tusche. After the first scraping of glue has dried, a second one is applied in exactly the same way. Any flakes of glue left on the tusche can be scraped off with your fingernail or a dull knife. When it is dry, the tusche is removed from the screen with mineral spirits or turpentine (again see Chapter 4), and any unwanted pinholes are filled with the glue solution. The screen can now be printed.

Lacquer can be used with the tusche in the same manner as glue to make a stencil that can be used with either water- or oil-based paints. There are also other combinations of two resist materials that serve the same purpose. Hot wax or liquid wax emulsion can be dripped or painted on the screen as the temporary resist, with glue or lacquer used as the second or permanent resist. The glue formula for a glue blockout stencil mentioned earlier in this chapter can be used for the temporary resist—it is a little more concentrated than the glue applied over tusche—with lacquer for the permanent resist. Stove enamel, asphaltum varnish, pressure-sensitive decals, press-type letters, and masking tape can serve as temporary resists with either glue or lacquer as the permanent resists.

Rubber cement or, better still, Maskoid has great possibilities as the temporary resist with lacquer as the permanent resist. Maskoid is a rubber-based product used by commercial illustrators and can be purchased at most art stores. It can be thinned with distilled water and has the advantage of drying quickly. It can be peeled off the screen if a mistake is made. Maskoid can be handled very freely and spontaneously because, unlike most other first resists, it does not need a second coat. It will give a very fine line and can be applied with a brush, bamboo pen, strip of cut cardboard, crumpled paper, or sponge. Maskoid tends to coagulate in a brush, but this can be prevented by lathering a little soap in the brush before it is used. After the stencil design has been finished, the brush and pen can be cleaned in soapy water. The screen is coated with lacquer for a second permanent resist, and the Maskoid is rubbed off with the fingers to create the stencil.

Another interesting method of producing a washout resist is to combine a temporary blockout with a permanent photographic emulsion. Clean the screen thoroughly, then apply the gelatin emulsion to the screen mesh in the manner suggested in Chapter 5; however, do *not* add the liquid sensitizer to the emulsion at this point. Because the emulsion is not sensitized, this process does not require a darkened room. After giving the screen two coats of the emulsion and allowing each coat to dry, paint your design on the underside of the screen mesh with black lacquer. After the lacquer is dry, carefully and quickly brush the sensitized emulsion on the *under surface of the screen only*. Be careful not to get it on the gelatin emulsion on the inside of the frame. Lay the frame flat (underside up) on the table and allow it to dry in that position. Then stand it in the light to expose it. In bright summer sunlight, only about five or six minutes will be needed. On dull winter days, several hours should elapse. You will need to experiment here. Some fluorescent lights will not affect the emulsion; photoflood lamps will, but are slower than bright sunlight. When the screen is fully exposed, take it to a sink and gently wash the *inside* of the screen fabric with water between 90 and 120 degrees. The unexposed emulsion under the lacquer design will float away taking most of the lacquer with it. Stubborn bits of lacquer and gelatin can be removed with lacquer thinner and warm water. If you are interested in the photographic process described later in this chapter, you will learn something by trying this simple version first. (See Chapter 8 for removal of the resist.)

After you acquire some confidence and skill with this form of stencil resist, you might try printing a single washout stencil that uses three different resists for each of three colors. With some skill in overprinting, many more colors than the original three can result. Carefully work out your design in detail in a sketch. Cover all of the areas to be printed with color number one on the inside of the screen mesh with Maskoid. Paint the areas to be printed with color number two on the screen mesh with two coats of tusche (Fig. 6–10). Paint all of the areas that are to print color three with two coats of glue. Then scrape the permanent resist, a lightly tinted lacquer, over all of the inside of the screen (again on the inside of the screen). Do not make it any heavier than necessary to cover the meshes still left open.

Now rub Maskoid off the screen mesh, and print the first color. After this color is printed, protect those parts of the screen that are to remain this color with the lightly tinted lacquer. If you do not cover all of color number one, you will increase the richness of your colors.

Next, from the underside of the frame (the printing side) remove the tusche resist with turpentine. You may have to do some rubbing from both sides to accomplish this. When it has been removed, print color number two. When finished, protect those areas you wish to leave as printed with the tinted lacquer. Part will be color number two only, and the rest will be color two printed over color one.

Finally, complete the design by removing the glue with hot water from the underside of the printing frame and printing the third color. The final resist is then removed from the screen with lacquer thinner. This is not a process for the beginner to attempt, but after you have gained a little experience and skill, it could be a challenge for you and it can produce some very interesting results.

Fig. 6–9. Liquid lithographic tusche is applied to the surface of the screen fabric with a brush.

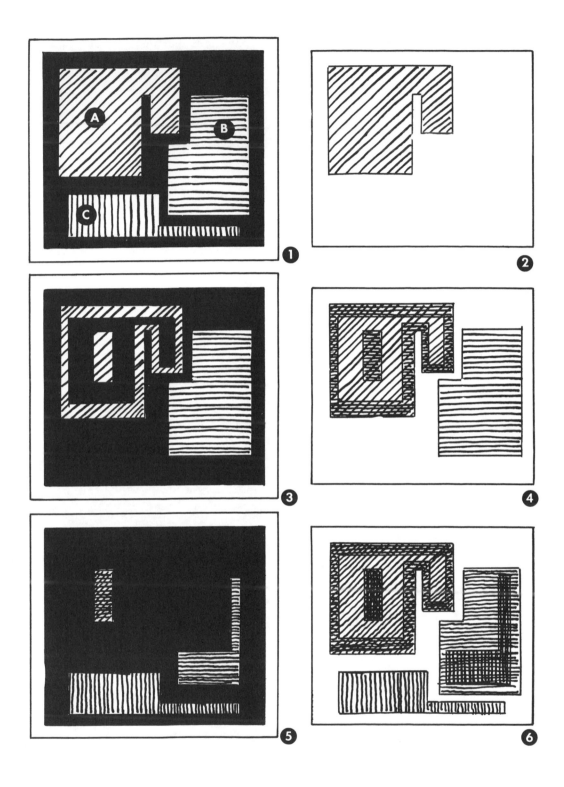

Fig. 6–10. This drawing shows how to create a six-color design using only one stencil with three different blockout resists and three colors of transparent ink. (1) First a Maskoid resist (A), a water-soluble glue resist (B), and a lacquer-soluble resist (C) are applied to the screen fabric; then a permanent blockout that will resist rubbing, water, and lacquer is applied over all. (2) The Maskoid is rubbed off and color number one (diagonal lines) is printed. (3) All but the outside edge and the central rectangle in the first-color area of the screen are now blocked out with the permanent resist and the water-soluble resist is washed off area B. (4) Color number two (horizontal lines) is now printed. (5) Additional areas of the screen that printed the first and second colors are blocked with the permanent resist and the lacquer-soluble resist is removed. (6) Color number three (vertical lines) is now printed. Where color two overprints color one, a fourth color is created; where color three overprints color two, there is a fifth color; and where color three overprints the first and second colors combined, there is a sixth color.

The Cut-Film Stencil

When, in 1929, Louis F. D'Autremont and A. S. Danemon brought out the first hand-cut film stencil, called Profilm, it revolutionized the commercial screen-process printing industry. Because the early Profilm was easy to use, it brought the screen-process print to the attention of artists and teachers throughout the country. For most, however, it was still a process for making school posters without involving an entire art class in every poster project. Even today, when there are many different types and brands of hand-cut film stencils, many screen printers still refer to any cut-film stencil as "Profilm." Because of the sharp, clean-cut image that it produces, the cut-film stencil is widely used by commercial printers, artists, and designers.

We are not going to repeat the rudiments of the process given in Chapter 4. Instead, some suggestions that might make each step a little easier will be given. Basically a cut-film resist is a stencil that is a laminate of at least two materials. First there is a backing, frequently a heavy grade of good wax paper. Since wax paper is affected by heat and humidity, some of the newer stencils are bonded to clear acetate. The film layer, which is what actually becomes the permanent resist on the screen fabric, is made from at least three different materials. The film of lacquer is still most common, but recently lacquer-proof films adhered with a special adhesive and water-soluble films adhered with water have become available. The earliest Profilm was made of shellac on a wax-paper base and was adhered with a warm iron. This was more difficult to use than contemporary film but had one advantage over it. A single knife cut would not reseal itself when the film was adhered, and very fine lines could be cut and printed. Such film is very difficult to obtain today. Films come in a variety of colors, and different film cutters prefer different colors. Eye strain and the ability to distinguish the colors of the original sketch through the film are reasons to choose a particular color.

A simple design is fairly easy to cut, and most beginners who observe a few precautions can do it satisfactorily. But professional film cutting is a highly skilled part of the commercial screen industry, and good film cutters are in great demand. The shortage of highly trained film cutters has accelerated the use of the more complicated photographic screen resists.

The film is placed over the sketch to guide the cutting. Since the knife should not cut through the backing, the sketch will be protected. Some designers like to arrange cut paper under the film, then cut the stencil following ideas suggested by the shapes.

There are a few precautions to observe in cutting. Cleanliness is paramount. Any grease or foreign material on the surface of the film will make the adhering step much more difficult, especially with water-adhering films, which are more susceptible to grease. Hands should be kept clean and should not touch the working surface of

Fig. 6–11. A scooper cutter is used in cutting lacquer-film stencils to remove thin lines from the film.

the film except when it is unavoidable. Keeping a clean sheet of paper between your hand and the film is a good practice.

There are many different types of stencil knives. The ordinary single-blade stencil knife with the blade inserted into an aluminum handle is most frequently used. There are also double-bladed knives to cut both sides of a line at once, and circle or compass cutters. One of the most useful of the special knives is a scooper cutter, which comes in three sizes for three different widths of cuts. The blade is a small circle of cutting steel, and the cutting edge is at the inside of the bottom of the metal loop. The round blade literally scoops the film off its backing. It can be used very rapidly and gives a loose, sketchy line (Fig. 6–11). Also available and quite popular is a knife with a swivel blade that revolves as you cut curves. All knives must be kept sharp as a surgeon's scalpel. An excellent investment would be two sharpening stones, one a reddish India stone for sharpening the knife edge, and the other a white Arkansas stone for final honing of the blade. Both stone surfaces are lubricated for sharpening with a few drops of light machine oil. When the knife edge becomes dull, too much pressure is necessary to cut cleanly through the film, which distorts the backing sheet. This does not permit good contact between the film and the screen mesh during the adhering process. Adhering becomes almost impossible if distortion is severe. Too much pressure will make a sharp knife cut through the film backing, which also presents adhering problems. Actually, a very light pressure should be sufficient. In many cases, the pressure exerted only by the natural weight of the blade and handle will do the job. One way to test the pressure is to rub your fingers lightly over the film backing. If you can feel ridges where the knife has cut, you are likely to have trouble adhering the film.

Fig. 6–12. (Reproduced in full color between pages 16 and 17.) Textile pattern composed of images in a light-sensitive film stencil made with a dry-copier transparency from current press cuttings produces a social commentary banner. (By Bobette Heller)

Cutting must be done on a smooth, hard surface. A sheet of glass or Formica works best, although the cutting blade will get dull and require more frequent sharpening. Scarred and marred surfaces and those with wood grain are to be avoided. Overcutting the line slightly is a good practice. This will ensure good clean corners and allow you to peel off the unused film more easily. The slight cut that extends into the film area will seal when the film is adhered. Often, if a section of the film is inadvertently removed, it can be replaced with the heat and pressure of your finger or the judicious application of a small amount of rubber cement thinned with 50 per cent rubber-cement thinner. Use a dull knife, an old ballpoint pen or a pair of tweezers for peeling off the film parts to be discarded. Instead, some designers place small lacquer-film pieces in a bottle with a little lacquer thinner to dissolve into a syrupy liquid that can be used to repair the printing screen. A wood-burning tool can be used to remove portions of the lacquer film. Small holes can be made with the tip, and broad areas can be removed with the side. Great care must be exercised to avoid burning the backing. Large areas where the film is removed will adhere more easily if a small hole is cut through the backing to allow air to escape. Film that has been stored too long gets dark and is more difficult to cut and to adhere, especially films with wax-paper backing. After the cutting is finished, roll up a small ball of masking tape with the adhesive to the outside of the ball. This is an excellent device for picking up any bits of cut film that have not been removed from the surface. If you are not going to adhere the cut film immediately, put it in a large envelope or file folder to keep it from gathering dust.

The screen fabric must be absolutely clean and free from grease before the film is adhered. Clean it with trisodium phosphate followed by a 5 per cent acetic acid solution (vinegar will work) and then rinse off the acid with cold water. Just before adhering the lacquer-film stencil, wipe the frame and screen mesh with a rag dampened slightly with lacquer thinner to remove all dust particles and prepare the mesh for the adhering process. Place a heavy piece of cardboard on a table. The cardboard should be a little larger than the cut film and smaller than the printing area inside the frame. Now put the cut-film stencil film side up on the cardboard to force the film and mesh to contact firmly. Position the frame with the mesh contacting the film and adhere them as suggested in Chapter 4. If the film does not adhere properly, it could be because the cutting pressure was too heavy, because there is too much humidity, or because the film is too old. If the problem is in the cutting, it is too late. Excessive humidity can be corrected by drying the film carefully in front of an electric room-heater. Adhering old film can be facilitated by rubbing a solution of xylene (a solvent for rubber cement) on both sides of the cut film. It will not damage the film, and it will loosen the rubber cement that adheres the film to the backing. Xylene is a hazardous chemical; check label

precautions before use. After the adhered film has dried for twenty to thirty minutes (depending on conditions of humidity), carefully peel off the backing (see Chapter 4). The film is now ready for printing.

Lacquerproof films and those adhered with water are handled in exactly the same manner. Follow the manufacturer's directions.

See Chapter 8 for removal procedures.

The Photo-Emulsion Resist

In recent years, the use of photogelatin emulsions in the screen printing process has added to the already great versatility of the medium. There are basically two methods of using a photogelatin emulsion. In the *direct method*, the emulsion is scraped in liquid form on the screen fabric and dried. The entire process takes place right on the screen mesh. In the *transfer method*, the emulsion is placed on some other support and not transferred to the screen mesh until the image is completed. Actually, there are two different transfer methods. In the *single transfer*, sensitizing the emulsion, exposing it, and washing out are done on a film backing, usually of acetate. The image is then transferred to the screen mesh for printing. In the *double transfer*, the emulsion is sensitized on the support it comes on. It is then transferred to a temporary support such as a sheet of Mylar. The emulsion is then exposed (often while wet), washed out, and the image transferred to the screen mesh.

The photo-emulsion resist is based on the principle that ordinary photogelatin to which a sensitizer like ammonium bichromate has been added becomes water insoluble when exposed to light. Those parts of the gelatin emulsion that have not been affected by the light remain water soluble and wash off to create the image.

The emulsion can be exposed to the light and the image produced by a number of methods. The simplest is to place opaque objects directly on the emulsion to prevent light from reaching it. Pieces of opaque paper or cardboard, semiopaque woven materials, threads and yarn, leaves, sticks, plant stems, paper clips, bolts, and many other things can be used here. This is probably the most direct way of creating an image. Even the dry-copy machines found in most offices can be used. These employ various heat-transfer processes to produce transparencies that can be used with the photogelatin emulsion resist. Halftone images from the printed page can be converted into two-dimensional motifs. Follow manufacturers' directions for making these transparencies. This process suggests great design possibilities. Designs can be painted on clear acetate sheets with heavy opaque black paint. For larger designs, photo masking films with adhesive backing can be applied with ease to the acetate. In addition, a film acetate can be made with orthochromatic photomechanical film such as Kodalith. This is a very high-contrast medium-speed film that can be exposed

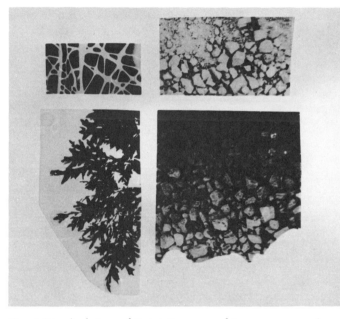

Fig. 6–13. A photographic negative exposed in a camera can be projected or enlarged on Kodalith film to produce a positive transparency with high contrast.

Fig. 6–14. Kodalith positive transparencies to which the hand script was added were exposed on presensitized screen-process film for this print. ("Through the Countryside," by Caroline Hunkel Kitelinger)

directly in the camera to produce a high-contrast negative. It can also be used to create a large high-contrast positive when a suitable negative is used in an enlarger (Fig. 6–13 and 6–14). If an image with halftones is to be produced, a negative must be made with an 85-line halftone screen (this means that there are 85 dots and white spaces per linear inch). Anything finer than that in the enlarger will cause problems in the printing process. The halftone screen negative then can be put in the enlarger to produce a positive on Kodalith film. Both the painted acetates and the photographic positive are placed in contact with the emulsion to produce the resist screen.

There are a number of light-sensitive photo-emulsion screen films produced by commercial companies that are fast enough to be used directly in a copy camera or an enlarger. For the serigrapher and the fabric designer, using these speedier films with an enlarger presents many opportunities. Being able to change the scale, size, and focus of the image makes for great design flexibility. In addition, objects can be distorted by varying the distance of the printing surface from the enlarging lens. The possibility of using only a very small section of a much larger image also opens new doors. Photographic positives can be used in the enlarger, as can small bits of actual objects like the wings of insects, leaves, tissue paper, and textured cloth. Slides, negatives, and objects can be enlarged and projected on to either Kodalith film or the high-speed photo-emulsion sensitized screen film.

As a graduate student in related art at the University of Wisconsin, Patricia K. Mansfield produced interesting textile patterns using photo-emulsion film resists and an enlarger. She found that exposure factors, developing procedures, and manipulative inventiveness are part of the necessary experimentation before satisfactory results can be achieved. The process offers endless challenges to the serious designer. Mrs. Mansfield advocates the use of the enlarger as a tool for designing. Familiarity with its mechanical advantages and limitations is necessary. However, such familiarity can be gained by using and manipulating it in the search for design statements. It is one of the tools of our century, and contemporary designers need to become sensitive to and selective of the potentials lying within this photographic experience.

The range of decorative detail possible with the photo-emulsion resist can be easily seen in (Fig. 6–15). On the left side of the picture is a detail from a photograph of a found texture that was exposed on presensitized film with the enlarger. In the center is a bamboo fly swatter that was laid down directly on the gelatin film resist with the enlarger as the light source. At the right, a piece of metal lathe for wall construction was placed on the screen photo film and exposed, then printed over a background texture.

Probably the simplest, most direct way to produce a photo-emulsion screen resist is with transfer films. These can be used either for single transfer or double transfer. They vary in speed and in the amount of detail they give. There are many more available from screen-process supply houses than we could cover adequately, and each comes with descriptions and directions for use. You will need to choose and to experiment. While most large suppliers are geared to the needs of the screen-process industry, many will send sample kits if you want to try out a material. Some of the film companies also package small trial kits. But while transfer films are easiest and most direct to use, they are also the most expensive, and you may want to try the direct emulsion method instead.

In the direct method, you apply a liquid gelatin emulsion to your screen fabric. The emulsion can be sensitized in advance in the liquid form. This is the normal procedure, but it causes some difficulties. The sensitized screens must be dried in a darkened room and can be stored for only a few hours before they begin to deteriorate. However, the unsensitized emulsion can also be applied to the screen even in a light room, then dried and stored for a reasonable period of time. When you wish to use it, it can be brushed with the sensitized emulsion and dried in a dark room just before exposure. This is a little more convenient.

Again, many varieties of photogelatin liquid emulsions are available from commercial supply houses. If expense is no factor and you are not doing too many screen prints, these may be your best bet. They are very uniform and dependable, and they are less expensive than transfer films. However, the photogelatin emulsion formula given

Fig. 6–15. Textile prints made with presensitized screen-process film are displayed on a wall. (By Patricia K. Mansfield)

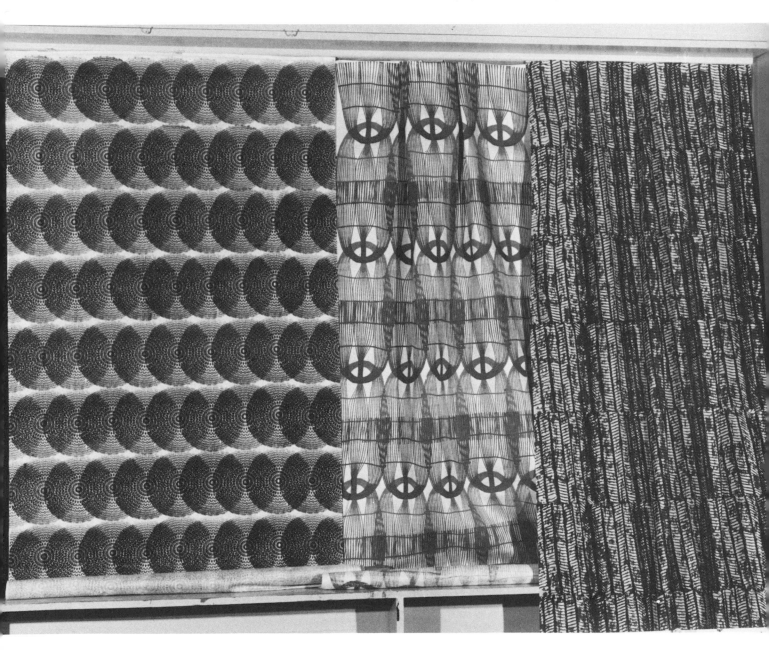

91

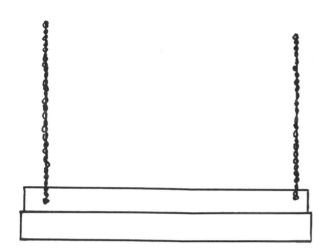

Fig. 6–16. In exposing a light-sensitive emulsion resist on a table with the light source suspended above the screen (1), the light source must be large enough and high enough to cover the entire screen with even illumination. Fluorescent tubes are best, but photoflood bulbs (which require longer exposure) can be used. A light box especially made for exposing light-sensitive emulsion resists (2) contains eight 4-foot fluorescent light tubes (A) spaced 6 inches below a sheet of heavy plate glass (B) that supports the emulsion. A 40-watt yellow insect bulb (C) can be placed in the box for illumination when materials are adjusted before exposure.

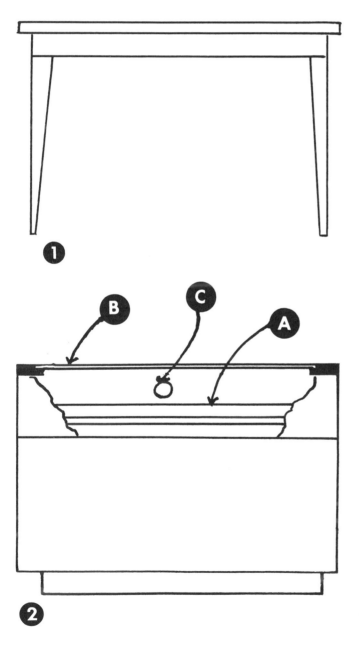

in Chapter 5 is not too difficult to make or use, and its cost is practically negligible.

Here are a few miscellaneous suggestions about photo-emulsion resists that might reduce some problems. Get in the habit of using rubber or disposable plastic gloves during most of the process. Many of the chemicals used are very strong and can burn or cause skin eruptions. When mixing solutions, use distilled water whenever possible; this is not always necessary, but occasionally a failure can be traced to something foreign in the water supply.

Sensitizing solutions should always be kept cool—no warmer than 60 degrees. Warmer temperatures will tend to oxidize some of the chemical and destroy part of its potential even during mixing. Too-warm sensitizer applied to dry gelatin may damage the gelatin. When you are adding a dye color to the gelatin to increase its visibility on the screen, purple, green, or blue are best; other colors might alter exposure times. When washing out the exposed gelatin, use a gentle spray. The water should be no cooler than 90 degrees and no hotter than 115 degrees. When mixing the gelatin emulsion, do not heat the water over 167 degrees.

Exposure times will probably have to be determined to suit your own needs. Generally speaking, the direct gelatin photo emulsion needs a longer exposure than most of the transfer films. But the exposure time depends on the kind of light source, the distance between the light source and the emulsion, and the capacity of the objects, films, or acetates that you are using for your image. Most commercial products give definite exposure suggestions. There are two ways to set up the light source. The preferred way is a light box, but a light suspended above the emulsion will also work (Fig. 6–16). In a glass-covered light box containing a bank of eight 4-foot-long 40-watt white fluorescent tubes about 6 inches from the emulsion, the average exposure will range between four and eight minutes for most emulsions except high-speed ones. If a No. 2 photoflood bulb (equivalent to about 700 watts of light) is suspended about 2 feet above the emulsion, exposures of twenty to forty minutes will be called for. But you will have to make exposure adjustments to suit your own situation. If you get a good clean image, the exposure time is correct. If the image cannot be seen at all or washes away in the warm water bath, then the exposure time is too short. If the image cannot be washed out or the fine line details are filled in, the exposure is too long. These results assume that the wash water has correct temperature and force. Too-cold water will not wash out the image; it will only harden it. Too-warm water will dissolve all of the gelatin. Excessive water pressure will also destroy the image. This process takes skill, but it is not as difficult as it sounds.

It is also important to protect the emulsion from light halation during exposure. This can be done by placing a matte black cloth or cardboard with the emulsion-and-image sandwich. There must also be pressure on the image so that it is held firmly against the emulsion. For stencil resists that are exposed from above, a heavy piece of good-quality plate glass will do the job. Stencil resists exposed on a light box can be weighted down with bricks on a piece of plywood with foam-rubber padding underneath Fig. 6–17).

One of the major handicaps of photo-emulsion resists is that most are susceptible to water damage from water-based inks and particularly from water-based dyes, especially in the direct emulsion method. You can purchase a direct-method liquid emulsion produced for use with water-based inks; but some cannot be removed from the screen mesh, so check. The transfer films seem to hold up a little better, but they too are subject to water deterioration.

Several companies sell preparations that can be applied to harden emulsions and make them more water resistant. Use them with care, because with some the stencil will not come off the screen fabric after use. A new fabric has to be stretched before a new design can be made. If the destruction of the screen fabric is no problem, then the resist can be made impervious to water by brushing the inside of the stencil with a synthetic enamel. Before the enamel has dried, the underside of the screen fabric is rubbed with a cloth dampened in mineral spirits. This will quickly clean all of the wet enamel out of the screen meshes. When the first enamel coat is dry on the inside of the frame, the process is reversed. The enamel is brushed on the underside of the screen fabric, and the printing meshes are cleaned from the inside with a cloth dampened in mineral spirits. This will protect the screen very well, but the screen fabric will have to be replaced for a different pattern. A somewhat less predictable method is to use lacquer on the inside of the screen mesh, cleaning it with lacquer thinner, and shellac on the underside, cleaning it with alcohol. This gives a fair degree of protection, and the substances can be removed from the screen, saving the screen fabric for future use.

See Chapter 8 for removing photo-emulsion resists.

Fig. 6–17. The top part of this drawing shows the top-to-bottom sequence for placing various materials for safe exposure of a light-sensitive emulsion when the light source is suspended above: light source (A); screen frame if emulsion is in the screen fabric (B); heavy piece of clear plate glass (C); acetate containing opaque materials for the design (D); light-sensitive emulsion (E); black paper to prevent light halation during exposure (F); table support (G). The lower section of the drawing shows the proper sequence when the light source is in a light box below the emulsion: screen frame if the emulsion is in the screen fabric (A); bricks or other heavy objects to weight down the various layers to guarantee good contact (B); thin sheet of plywood (C); black paper or thin sheet of black foam rubber to prevent halation during exposure (D); light-sensitive emulsion (E); acetate containing opaque materials for the design (F); heavy plate glass top of the light box (G); light source (H); light box (I).

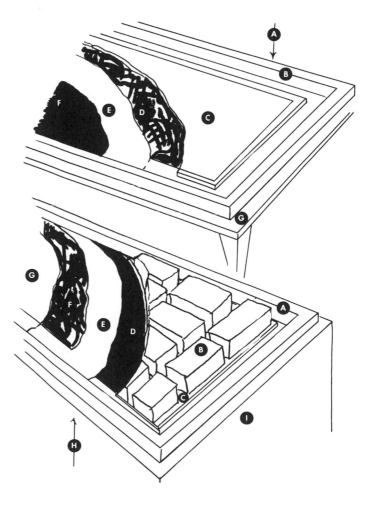

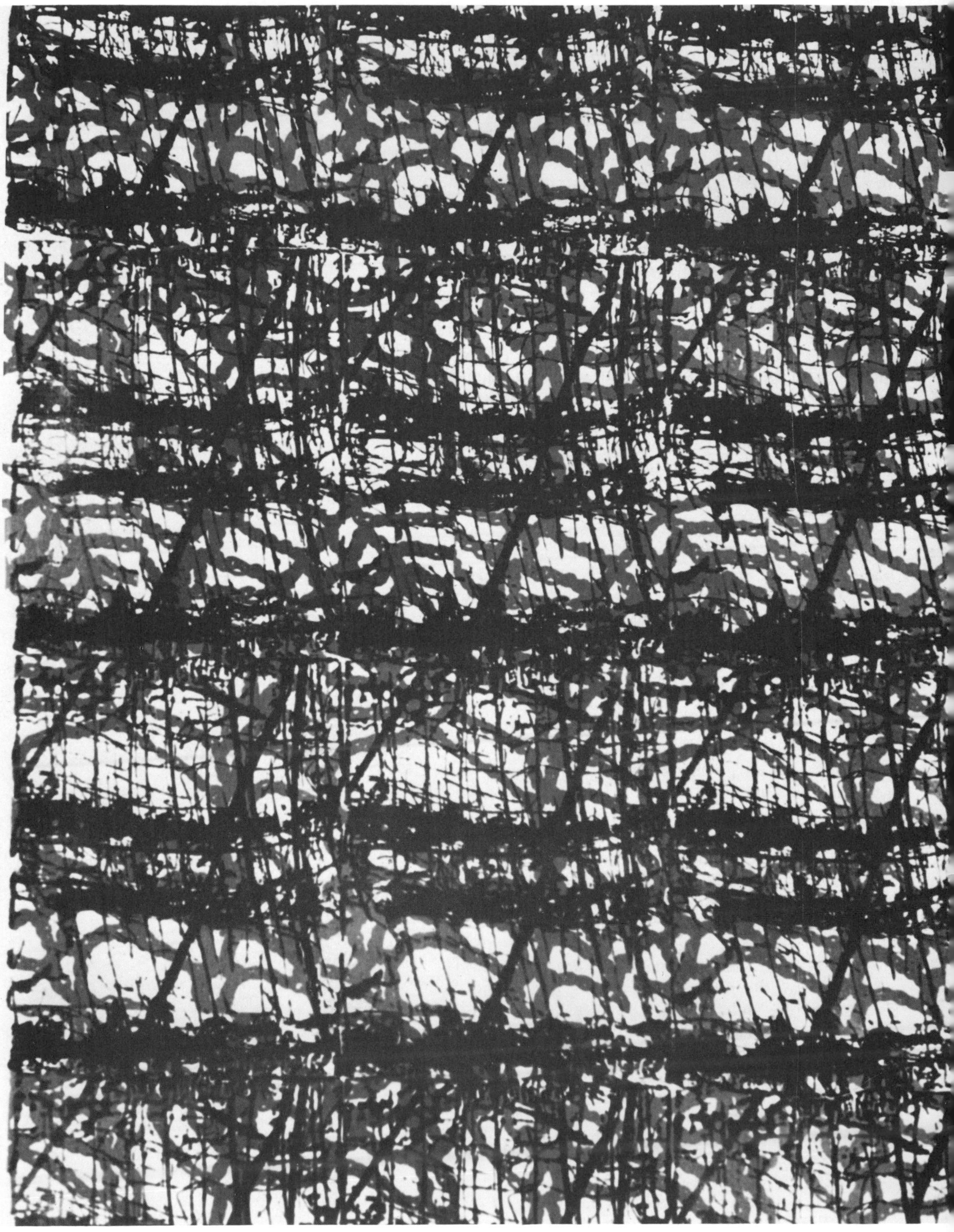

7. TECHNIQUES FOR PRINTING

In this chapter we will discuss further techniques for constructing a printing board and frame as well as include some information about inks, paints, and dyes that can be used and what fabrics and papers will accept printing. In addition, the actual techniques of using printing media, keying the screen, pulling the squeegee, and drying the results will be given. Printing techniques mentioned in preceding chapters will not be repeated.

Construction of the Frame and Printing Base

In Chapter 4 we suggested that clear pine should be used for the construction of the basic wood frame. But other woods that are sometimes used are spruce, mahogany, basswood, and boxwood. English screen printers frequently make their frames from sycamore and beech. For frames smaller than 15 by 20 inches, 1⅛- by 1⅛-inch lumber is recommended. Frames from 15 by 20 inches to 30 by 40 inches should be made from 1⅝- by 1⅝-inch lumber.

The butt joint suggested in Chapter 4 is the simplest joint to make, but there are a number of other ways of joining four pieces of frame lumber together, most of which (miter, rabbet, end lap, dovetail) are preferred to the butt joint because of their greater strength (Fig. 7–2).

Fig. 7–1. Two screens were used to produce this print, which was designed with bark fibers and a lace doily. (By Timothy J. McIlrath)

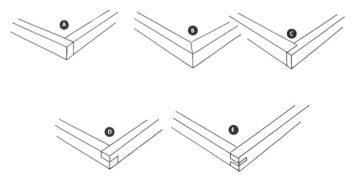

Fig. 7–2. This drawing shows some of the various types of end joints that can be used in screen frames: butt joint (A); mitered joint (B); rabbet joint (C); end-lap joint (D); dovetail joint (E).

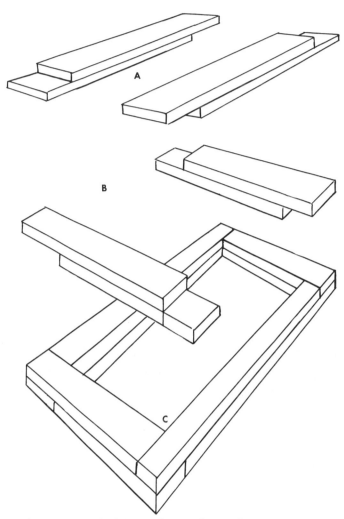

Fig. 7–3. One method for making a frame if your carpentry skill is limited is with end-lap joints. For each side, two pieces of lumber of equal length are glued together with one piece extended on each end a distance equal to the width of the lumber used. The drawing shows two assembled side pieces (A), two assembled end pieces (B), and the completely assembled frame (C).

Fig. 7–4. An end-lap joint can be strengthened with an angle iron (A). Drop-pin hinges make attaching the frame to the printing board fairly simple. The drop-pin (B) is removed to show the female section of the hinge (C) on the frame and the male section (D) on the printing board. On the other end of this side of the screen the arrangement should be reversed; that is, the male section should be on the frame and the female on the printing board.

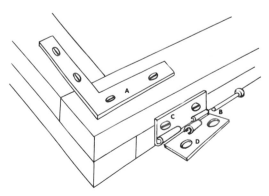

If you have limited carpentry skill and a minimum of equipment, you might try the version of the end-lap joint (shown in Fig. 7–3) calling for two pieces of lumber on each side. If you do, it would be wise to strengthen the joints with angle irons (Fig. 7–4).

The methods for constructing a printing board for textiles and for keying the frame to it were discussed in Chapter 5. A temporary surface for textile printing can be made by carefully padding a table top or flat board with smooth semisoft materials and taping them to the table instead of stapling them.

In serigraphy, a simple drop-pin hinge used to fasten the screen to the printing surface is a good idea because it makes it possible to use several printing frames with a single base. Be sure to put the male and female halves of one hinge on the base (Fig. 7–5). If you are setting up a permanent printing studio, a strong, sturdy table makes the best base. Then you will need to screw the two halves of a drop-pin hinge to each screen so that it fits the one set of hinges on the table. In a somewhat better way of fastening the frame to the printing base, the frame is hinged to a length of the same-size wood used in its construction, which is then bolted to the table or printing board with carriage bolts and wing nuts (Fig. 7–6). Ordinary hinges or even a piano hinge can be used, since the frame is removed from the board with the extra piece of wood attached. This arrangement is a bit steadier, and it allows the printing frame to be shimmed up at both ends when thick materials are being printed (Fig. 7–7).

There was a time when the silk-screen artist purchased heavy belt rubber and made his own squeegee. Squeegees can still be improvised from stiff, thin pieces of cardboard or wood, but the most practical procedure is to acquire a good commercially produced squeegee. The kind made for two hands (you pull the squeegee toward you or push it away, using both hands on the wood part of the blade) is recommended because it is easy to work and gives greater control. But also popular with many printers are one-handed squeegees (Fig. 7–8). These have a vertical handle that is grasped firmly in either the right or the left hand depending upon the direction of the stroke and, usually, is passed from side to side in front of the printer.

The blade of a squeegee is rated in durometers to indicate flexibility. A very soft blade is approximately 45 durometers, while a hard one is 80 durometers. A blade for textiles is usually thin and soft (between 45 and 50 durometers). A soft blade forces more dye paste or textile ink into the weave of the textile. The blade used for most serigraphs is 50 to 60 durometers, or about medium in flexibility. For hard, sharp lines, intricate details, and very thin applications of ink, hard blades up to 80 durometers may be used. Hard blades are also used on nonabsorbent surfaces. Formerly all blades were of natural rubber, but plastic blades have come on the market recently. While they are more expensive, they are tough and need minimum sharpening. They also clean easily. Some firms identify the hardness of the blade by color:

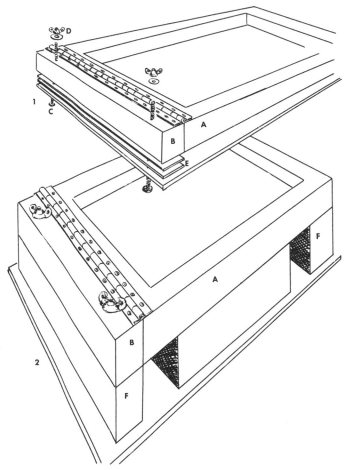

Fig. 7–5. Reversing the male and female parts of the hinge on the two sides of the frame means a saving in hardware. Each time you make a new frame simply attach the two parts of one hinge to it to fit the hinge arrangement on the printing board.

Fig. 7–7. With the printing frame (A) attached to an extra block of wood (B), which in turn is bolted to the printing surface (C) with carriage bolts and wing nuts (D), materials of varying thicknesses can be printed. For example, if you wish to print a thin sheet of metal, a thickness or two of cardboard (E) inserted under the block of wood (B) will raise the frame the necessary distance. If you wish to print something very thick, such as a box, a block of wood (F) with holes drilled for the carriage bolts is used. (If a box being printed is cardboard, it may need a second block of wood (F) placed under the other end of the printing frame to protect the box from the printing pressure).

Fig. 7–6. An even better way of fastening the screen frame to the printing surface is to bolt an extra block of wood (A) the same height as the screen frame to the printing surface with carriage bolts (B) and to attach the frame to the block with a piano hinge (C).

Fig. 7–8. Squeegees may be either one-handed (A) or two-handed (B). A piece of wood (C) or dowels (D) attached to the squeegee will prevent it from falling into the ink during the printing process.

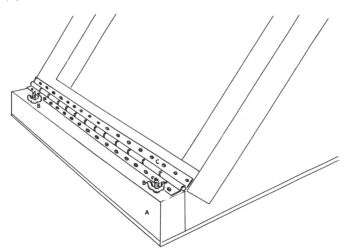

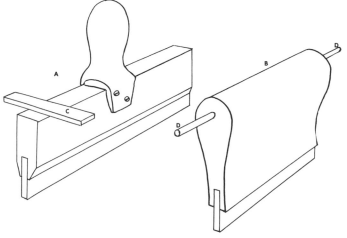

gray for hard, black for medium, amber for soft.

There are five or six different types of edges on squeegee blades. The one most frequently used by the serigrapher is sharp and square. With use it may round off or develop small nicks. This will give blurred and uneven printing images, and the nicks will cause streaks in the color areas. The blade will need to be sharpened with a fine sheet of sandpaper. Rub evenly and smoothly. Textile printers on the other hand will find that a blade edge that is basically square but slightly rounded will deposit more ink or dye paste on a textile. For fine printing and intricate details blades that are pointed or shaped like a chisel are used.

Fig. 7–9. Nails driven into the ends of a squeegee will also prevent it from falling into the ink. The squeegee is rested on the sides of the frame when not in use.

Some of the newer squeegee models have removable handles. A worn blade can be replaced or turned around and the other edge used. Blades should always be thoroughly cleaned after use. They should be hung up in storage or stored flat or propped up on the handle. They should never rest on the rubber blade or be stored with anything pressing against the blade. To keep a squeegee from falling into the paint in the frame while printing, drive wooden dowels or small nails (Fig. 7–9) into each end.

The Screen Mesh

Silk has long been the most common screen mesh. While it is still widely used, other materials are also popular. Inexpensive and disposable screens can be made from organdy. They do not work very well with water-based paints and should be used only for small runs. They also sag after they have been cleaned a number of times. Nylon meshes have been gaining in popularity because of their ease of cleaning and their durability. Silk does not stand up under the strong chemicals used in some photographic methods. Copper, brass, bronze, and stainless-steel fabric meshes are used in commercial screen printing because they hold up well for very long runs. But their cost, the difficulty of stretching them on a frame, and their susceptibility to damage from small dents makes them impractical for most small-volume screen printers.

Silk fabrics are classified with a number that indicates the size of the mesh holes and an X to signify the strength of the weave. All screen silks are rated XX (double weight) as to strength. The following table gives mesh counts, which are the number of mesh holes per linear inch.

	Silk	Nylon		Silk	Nylon
1XX	48		13XX	127	
2XX	54		14XX	136	230
4XX	62		15XX	144	
6XX	73	157	16XX	152	240
7XX	81		17XX	160	
8XX	86		18XX	170	283
9XX	95		19XX	175	
10XX	106	185	20XX	180	306
11XX	114		21XX	185	
12XX	122		22XX	200	

Most serigraphers use grades between 10XX and 16XX. Generally speaking, 10XX is for heavier and coarser printing, and 16XX is used with photo stencils. When textiles are printed with pigment colors, meshes between 8XX and 10XX are used, while meshes between 10XX and 12XX are required for printing with dyes.

For a heavy impasto effect with a paper blockout resist, a mesh of 12XX is commonly used. Listed here are the mesh numbers required for various types of stencil resists.

Cut film	6XX-12XX	Photo halftone	.18XX-19XX
Paper blockout .	6XX-12XX	Photo (with	
Photographic	..10XX-16XX	detail) 14XX-16XX	
Glue blockout	.12XX-18XX	Washout resist .14XX-18XX	
Mimeograph		Acetate block-	
stencil	9XX-12XX	out 12XX-19XX	

Most screen fabrics are stretched by one of the two methods described in Chapter 5. If staples are not available, No. 4 carpet tacks can be used. Some European printers adhere the fabric to the frame by temporarily tacking it with thumbtacks, then giving the areas where the screen and frame are in tight contact three or four

coats of clear lacquer. When the lacquer has dried, the tacks are removed and the screen is sealed with tape (see Chapter 5). A variation of the cord-and-groove method used in Chapter 5 can be seen in Fig. 7–10. Four grooves are cut in the screen frame, and wooden bars are fitted into them. The silk is placed under the bars and pulled somewhat tight. The bars are then slowly screwed into the frame. This method gives a very tight screen, but it requires a little more skill to use. Regardless of how you stretch screen fabric, the stretching tool used by artists to stretch canvas is a very useful implement to have. After the fabric has been stretched, it should be washed (see Chapter 8).

Fig. 7–10. In this method of stretching a screen, which is particularly good for a wire or metal screen fabric, a groove is cut into the screen frame (A) with a table saw. Then the screen fabric (B) is laid over the frame, and thin strips of hardwood (C) with screw holes (D) previously drilled in them are positioned above the fabric over the grooves in the frame and carefully screwed down into the grooves.

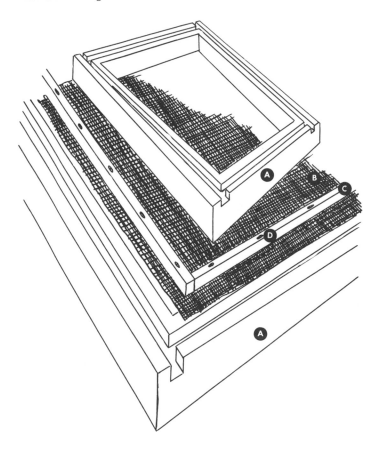

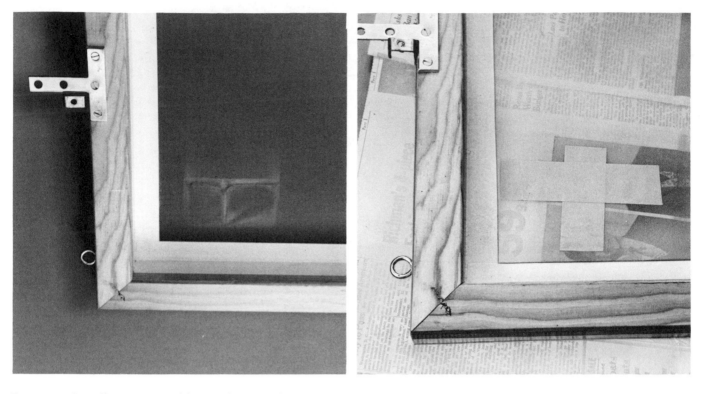

Fig. 7–11. A small tear in screen fabric can be repaired. First, the rip is covered on the underside with masking tape.

Fig. 7–12. Tape is then placed on the other side of the tear, and both sides are lacquered.

If a screen is punctured and the tear is not too large, it can be repaired. If adequate printing surface is left, the screen can be used for smaller designs. Carefully tape together the cut in the fabric on the underside with masking tape, then seal it on the inside with one or two coats of clear lacquer. After the lacquer has dried, cover that section with tape also, and lacquer the tape on both sides of the fabric with several coats (Figs. 7–11 and 7–12). The frame can now be used. A frame that develops a leak during printing can usually be temporarily repaired with masking tape. After the printing is finished, it is usually wise to tear off all of the tape around the leak, then completely reseal it with new tape. If a screen fabric becomes somewhat loose and saggy, you can sometimes continue to print by raising the printing surface with a sheet or two of cardboard. Place the cardboard, which should be smaller than the inside of the printing frame, under the print. This forces the print more tightly against the screen and takes up some of the slack in the fabric tension. In most cases this will only temporarily solve the problem of a loose screen fabric. Usually a new screen must be stretched.

Selecting and Preparing Printing Paints, Inks, or Dyes

Like other equipment for screen-process printing, the variety of paints, inks, and dyes available is almost overwhelming. We will not attempt to enumerate all of them, but instead list briefly and describe only those that are likely to be of most interest to the small-volume printer.

The paint used can be a kind that is very inexpensive and readily available, like the tempera paint formula in Chapter 3. Most screen-process supply houses also sell an inexpensive grade of water-based poster ink designed for school use that can be thinned and cleaned out of the screen with water. It is excellent for beginners if they do not wish any high degree of permanence. But you cannot use with it a screen resist that washes out with water.

Screen-process paints are thick and syrupy. Among them are the many varieties of *flat-type* or *poster colors*. They are not designed for outdoor use, but they can be used outdoors if given a coat of overprint varnish. These paints are made more transparent with transparent base, which also improves their printing quality. Frequently, toner base is mixed with the transparent base. The paints are thinned with mixing varnish and mineral spirits, and cleaned from the screen with paint thinner or mineral spirits.

High-gloss enamels come in two types: a fast-drying enamel that cannot be used outside without the protection of overprint varnish, and a synthetic or natural varnish with a high-gloss color. The second is suitable for outdoor use, and some types can even be baked on the printing surface at a temperature up to 350 degrees. Special thinners, transparent bases, and cleaning material should be those recommended by the manufacturers for most screen paints.

If you are looking for transparent colors, get one of the *transparent toner colors*. These are highly concentrated paints that are mixed with a crystal type of transparent base, which increases transparency without much loss of color value. Petroleum distillate or paint thinner is used to thin the paints and clean them off the screen.

If you are working with a screen resist not affected by lacquer, you can use *lacquer-based paints*. They are very brilliant and tend to dry rapidly. Special thinners are designed for use with them. If you cannot get a slow-drying thinner, add about a teaspoon of castor oil to a pint of the thinner you do get. This will prevent clogging of the mesh.

Contemporary serigraphers of the Op and Pop schools have been using *fluorescent inks*. Thinners, wash solutions, and transparent bases have been especially produced for these paints.

Designed for printing on glass but useful on paper as well are the *cellulose-based inks*. They are somewhat expensive but offer a wide range of brilliant colors. They print much thinner than do most oil-based inks, and they do not clog the mesh as quickly. Shellac screens cannot be used since the ink will dissolve the shellac. They require special cleaners, thinners, and transparent base.

A few more inks, primarily of interest to the serigrapher, are specialty products designed to print on plastics, acetates, and vinyl. There are inks that can be heated and used in the vacuum-forming process popular among Pop sculptors. Lithographers can use lithographic asphaltum to silk-screen photo images on lithographic stones, and etchers can do the same with an ink designed for the printing of etched electrical circuits. Ceramists can silkscreen photo images in a glaze on their ceramic objects before they fire them in the kiln.

For textile designers there are *water-based textile inks* that do not stiffen the cloth and that are fairly easy to use. Most need some form of heat setting but are reasonably color-fast if they are aged before washing and then washed with some care.

In addition, textile designers employ commercially manufactured *pigments in oil emulsion* and *pigments in water emulsion*, which are commonly used by some of the large screen-process textile firms on banners, T shirts, and sweat shirts. Although these inks are produced for textiles, they will stiffen the cloth slightly, but with some

experience and skill in the use of the thinners and extenders, the printer can reduce this stiffness. The inks are fairly easy to use and are quite color-fast and permanent. There are inks designed especially for awnings and similar outdoor banners and fabrics. Fluorescent textile inks offer striking effects, but they present some problems in pressing and laundering.

Since the mid-1950s, the use of dyes has increased rapidly. Any dye that can be produced in a paste form can be used in screen-process printing. The most useful dyes for the small-scale printer are acid dyes, basic dyes, direct dyes, disperse dyes, fiber-reactive dyes, household dyes, prepared vat dyes, and soluble vat dyes. These offer many avenues for the textile printer to explore. Each requires special handling, gives different results, and presents different difficulties.

Recently, textile printers have been working with fiber-reactive dyes, which are relatively easy to apply in paste form. The colors are fixed by development in a steam chamber or with a steam iron. They usually give brilliant transparent hues.

Probably the most critical part of screen printing is *mixing* the inks, dyes, and paints. Because the printing process considerably alters the final color, experience and only experience can give the printer the skill needed to mix color hues that will turn out to be what he wants. Colors are altered in drying, and they change a good deal depending upon the color, texture, and absorbency of the surface on which they are printed. Since even the experienced screen-process printer often can do no more than make an educated guess, it is wise to test-print a color before it is finally applied. Many printers have a series of screens as small as 4 by 6 inches with a permanent design on them (like squares, circles, or triangles, which lend themselves easily to overprinting color areas) for testing the colors to be used on a piece of the material to be printed. In this manner, the intensity, value, and shade of the color can be quite accurately judged. In addition, overprinting tests the relative transparency or opacity of the ink. If the color is incorrect, a small screen can be cleaned much more easily than a full-sized screen and the process repeated.

Mixed colors left over from previous printing runs should be very carefully checked for lumps and other inconsistencies before they are used. If there is any suspicion of foreign matter in the ink, strain it through cheesecloth or an old nylon stocking.

Screen-process paints come in pint, quart, and gallon cans; serious printers should purchase them by the quart. Most inks are available in half-pints, pints, quarts, and gallons. Transparent base, toner base, paint thinner or mineral spirits, and mixing varnish should be purchased by the gallon.

Only experience and participating perception will enable a textile printer to judge the quantity of textile paint or dye paste required. The amounts of ink needed depend on the size of the area receiving ink in each color run and and the absorbency and roughness of the fabric. Because textiles vary more in texture and ink absorbency than do most serigraphic papers, estimating the amount of ink needed is more difficult. The amount of pressure you use on the squeegee will also affect the amount of ink needed. It is advisable to mix at least one full cup of ink even for test runs or experimental purposes: better too much than too little. Unused color stores quite easily, or it can be blended with other colors.

Predicting the amount of paint needed in serigraphy is only a little easier. In both textile printing and serigraphy, it is important to mix about 3 ounces more paint than you will use, to prevent the squeegee from running out of ink before the printing run is finished. This overrun can be saved, so it is not lost. Mixing a color in the middle of a run is an unnecessary problem. Here is a rule of thumb for predicting the amount of paint needed to print one color run of a serigraph. Calculate roughly the area to be printed in square inches. Then, if your paper is average in texture and absorbency, and the humidity in the room, the pressure you place on the squeegee, and the angle of your stroke are normal, you can calculate that you will need roughly 3½ to 4 ounces of paint to cover about 100 square inches. This is estimated on an edition of twenty-five to thirty prints, including proof prints. If you add to that the 3 ounces allowed for overrun, you will need to mix 6½ to 7 ounces of printing ink to print an area of 100 square inches on each of twenty-five to thirty prints.

We are not going to discuss the mixing of colors to get certain hues, except to say that it will save ink if you follow the general rule of always adding dark colors to light colors and strong, intense colors to weaker, less intense colors; then, if you move slowly and cautiously, you will keep good control over your color mixing. Color mixing with screen-process paints, inks, or dyes is much like mixing any colors. If you need more help in color phenomena, get a good book on color theory and mixing. *Creative Color* by Faber Birren is recommended.

Besides mixing the pigments and dyes to produce the color desired, you can alter the basic nature of inks in a number of ways to affect the color. You can increase transparency with *transparent base*, which is made of aluminum stearate and varnish and has the consistency of soft butter. But since it often makes inks too thick and when dry causes ink to flake off, it is wise to mix with it a smaller amount of *toner base* (sometimes called *crystal base* or *clear base*). This transparent but syrupy solution improves the flexibility of the transparent base and helps prevent the flaking off of the paint when dry; in addition it has good binding qualities. Thick paint can be made thinner to improve its printing quality by adding a still smaller amount of *mixing varnish*. Therefore, a good mixture for increasing the transparency of serigraphic screen-process paints is approximately 25 ounces of transparent base, 17 ounces of toner base, and 8 ounces of mixing varnish. This can be kept in a container and mixed with the color to be printed to get the transparency required. Some should be mixed with all paints to improve their printing quality; about one part of this mixture can be

added to ten parts of most screen-process inks without reducing opacity to any noticeable degree.

If you wish the paint to dry more quickly, you can decrease the drying time with a *reducer*, and if you wish to slow down the drying time you can add a *retarder*. A retarder is necessary with some of the more volatile inks to prevent the screen from clogging on a day when the humidity is very low.

Proper printing consistency is important for a smooth printing operation. In both serigraphy and textile printing, the prepared ink should dribble slowly from the ink mixing stick. If it does not drop at all, it is too thick and needs the proper thinner. If it flows in a liquid stream from the stick, it is too thin and needs the proper thickener. Dye pastes tend to be a little more transparent and flow more readily.

Make test prints to become familiar with the number of passes of the squeegee required for each type of fabric. (Since only one pull of the squeegee is used in serigraphy, this test is not necessary.) Also experiment with the pressure on the squeegee to see how it will change the nature of the color. Observe carefully the effect that the base color of the cloth or paper has on the printed color. Colors cannot be evaluated until they have dried. Drying some paints can be speeded up with an electric hair dryer, but some dye pastes have to be developed in steam or chemicals before the final color can be judged.

When mixing fiber-reactive dyes for textile printing, a generous quart of printing paste or thickener can be prepared from the following: 1 teaspoon Calgon, 10 tablespoons urea, 1 teaspoon resist salt-L, 1 cup hot water, 3 cups cold water, and 3½ to 4 teaspoons Keltex (thickener). Dissolve the Calgon, urea, and resist salt-L in the 1 cup of hot water, then add the 3 cups of cold water. Stir or beat in 3½ teaspoons of Keltex for heavier cloth or 4 teaspoons for lightweight cloth with a hand beater until completely dissolved. This will make a basic thickener solution that can be stored in a closed container if refrigerated. Use 1 cup of the basic thickener at a time. To this 1 cup add the required Procion dyestuff: ½ teaspoon of Procion dye will give a pale value; 1 teaspoon will give a medium value; 2 teaspoons of Procion dye will give a dark value. Just before printing, dissolve 1 teaspoon of bicarbonate of soda in a small amount of water and add to the cup of thickener and dyestuff.

Since this dye paste has a thinner consistency than some of the prepared textile inks or paints, it is wise to make some test prints. Pressure on the squeegee, the amount of dye-paste mixture used in the printing frame, and the number of passes over the printing surface with the squeegee should be determined before starting on the final printing. You should also develop some of these test runs with a steam iron to determine the final color. Press for 5 minutes with a steam iron set at "steam," or at 285 degrees.

Discharging color from a fabric with a screen-print stencil is another way to design. A slightly different thickener (1 cup of hot water, ½ teaspoon of Calgon, and 2

Fig. 7–13. "Moons and Suns" is the title of this design, which is screen-printed on fabric. (By Mathilda V. Schwalbach)

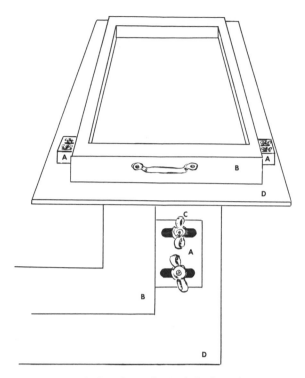

Fig. 7–15. Blocks of wood (*A*) bolted to the printing surface (*D*) with carriage bolts and wing nuts (*C*) hold the frame (*B*) in place accurately during printing. The slots in the blocks of wood allow necessary adjustments to be made.

Fig. 7–16. Metal clasp locks (*A*) fastened to both sides of the unhinged end of the printing frame (*B*) hold the frame securely against the printing board (*C*).

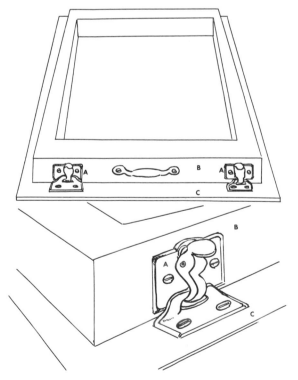

teaspoons of Keltex) is mixed, cooled, and then combined with an equal amount of chlorine bleach. This discharge solution has a good printing consistency. Because of the use of bleach in the paste, nylon mesh must be used for the screen. Cut lacquer-film stencils give a sturdy, hard-edged screen resist. Thorough washing and rinsing of the fabric is necessary to remove all of the discharge paste containing the bleach. Different fabric textures and fibers can be used, but it is not practical to use fabrics that are 100 per cent wool or silk, since the bleach in the paste will deteriorate the fibers.

Timothy J. McIlrath, who developed this process while a graduate teaching assistant in related art at the University of Wisconsin, has produced exhibition pieces of professional quality with the process (Fig. 7–14). He has used solid-color fabrics in blue, navy, brown, and black. When the discharge patterns have been printed, the original cloth colors are bleached to various subtle, earthy, frosty hues.

Correct Register Assures Printing Accuracy

To key or register a print in serigraphy and textile printing merely means that some device is used to assure that the printing frame comes down on the material to be printed in *exactly the same place* each time. This is not so important in a one-color serigraph. It is, however, essential in multicolor serigraphs and all fabrics that repeat a design. If the printer wishes to achieve an intuitive and random register, this is perfectly legitimate and can be exciting in its results. But he should be able to register a print accurately and consistently. Only then will he be skilled enough to exercise the amount of control needed even for a random print register.

There are two factors in controlling register. One is the permanently fixed printing frame and the other the adjustable parts where adaptations are possible. In serigraphy, the fixed instrument is the printing board with the hinged printing frame. Check to be absolutely sure that all of the permanently fixed parts of the printing frame and surface are rigidly attached. Check the hinges and bolts to be sure that they are tight. A device that will hold the frame in exactly the same place each time it comes in contact with the printing board is illustrated in Fig. 7–15. Slotted wood blocks are screwed to the printing board on each side of the printing frame. The blocks can be adjusted so they fit tightly against each side of the printing frame. When the board is brought down in contact with the printing paper, it is then held in place. There are special printing-frame locks that can be purchased from screen-process supply houses. They hold the unhinged end of the printing frame securely against the printing surface (Fig. 7–16).

In fabric printing, the permanent fixed part is the long printing board with metal key rails along one or both sides. The adjustable parts are the sliding bolts on each

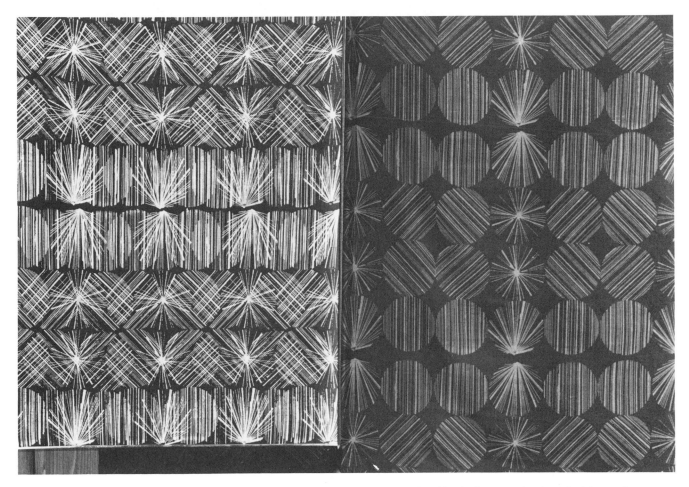

Fig. 7–14. (Reproduced in full color between pages 16 and 17.) This textile print was produced by discharging color from the fabric with a stencil. ("Morning Snow," by Timothy J. McIlrath)

of the side rails and the screw eyes at the end of each printing frame. See Chapter 5 for details on how these are used to register fabric for printing. In the printing of a serigraph, first adjustments will have to be made to take care of the thickness of the printing stock.

The two most important factors in correct print register are the register tabs on the printing surface and the register marks on the screen resist. For basic instructions in placing these, see Chapter 4. When heavier paper is used, the tabs must be made out of a piece of cardboard that is just a little bit thinner than the printing stock. A metal tab is nailed over the cardboard tab so that there is about a quarter of an inch overhang (Fig. 7–17). Register tabs should not be positioned under the frame so they press against the screen mesh while printing. If this is unavoidable, then smooth them with emery paper. The silk must also be protected with masking tape. This is most important when the metal tabs are used.

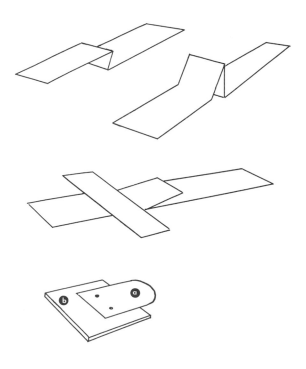

Fig. 7–17. For printing paper and thin cardboard, keying tabs made by folding gummed paper or masking tape are satisfactory. For anything thicker, nail a thin plastic or metal tab (a) placed on a piece of cardboard (b) the same thickness as the material to be printed onto the printing surface. If the tab is metal, it must have no sharp or rough edges.

Printing the Color Runs

The climax of the screen-print process is in the actual production of the print. Here is where you find the excitement. For everything up to this point has been conjecture, ideas, hopes. Now the unpredictability of a successful realization is what often keeps you printing late into the night. Of course, successful results are stimulating, but the creative printer should be ready to accept the more frequent failure. For when you are in search of that indefinable essence of a really successful creative effort, technical success often falls far short of the goal. Technical success should, with experience, be expected, but that certain "something" is much more elusive. But it is this very search that, in itself, has its own rewards. So, let us talk about the printing of the image.

The design that is on the screen resist can be changed in many ways in the printing process. In textile printing there are even more avenues open for creative interpretation in the printing process. Textile printers should deliberately experiment with printing a pattern in a variety of ways; after all, in no other textile design field can you experiment as easily. Different color harmonies can be attempted. The motif can be printed in a number of different arrangements and sequences. The design can be printed in part or in whole, reversed, or turned. Pressure on the squeegee can be varied in passing it across the screen. Paint can be added for gradual color changes. All of these suggest that the textile printer who does not print creatively is, indeed, not fully utilizing the process. The serigrapher has almost equal opportunities to be creative in the application of ink to paper. However, because he is normally not dealing with a repetitive unit and is working with fixed printing frame and board, he has a few more limitations.

Screen-process printers must first of all think of the transparency and opacity of the colors and develop a general scheme for the printing sequence of colors. This is necessary because whether a red is printed over a blue or a blue over a red makes a difference. The relative transparency or opacity of each greatly affects the color that results.

The printing operation can be performed by a single printer, if he is organized and able to keep his hands clean during the operation. However, it is much simpler when two printers work together. One sticks with the printing and handles the ink because he is liable to have soiled hands. The other handles the paper, registers it on the printing board, removes it from under the frame after the color has been applied, and stacks it in the drying rack. He must keep his hands clean. Small fabrics can be printed quite easily by one person. But almost all fabrics printed on a wide board need two printers to operate the squeegee, passing it from one side to the other in a smooth, rhythmic operation. Skilled screen printing looks deceptively easy; some experience is needed to develop the skill.

In large textile printing plants there are basically two methods of printing. One is a two-man operation on a very long table (150 to 200 feet long). The team works down the table length, printing every other unit in the first color. Then they print the intervening unit. This process is repeated for each color used in the design. The fabric hand-printed on a long table retains that subtle characteristic of a hand-produced object, the living human quality that many people prize. On the other hand, there are automatic screen-printing machines that use a much smaller table and can be operated by only one man. Such a machine can print 300 yards in one hour with an accuracy of 1/50,000 of an inch.

In hand printing there are basically two approaches in the number of screens used. Most serigraphers use only one screen. When the first color is printed, the screen resist is removed and a new one is added. In this process an edition could fail somewhere along the way: since all of the previous screen resists have been destroyed, there is no turning back except to start over completely. Textile designers, because they generally use fewer colors, can produce a separate frame for each resist used. This allows almost unlimited variation with the same basic pattern. In addition, the entire set of frames can be stored and the printed yardage duplicated or re-created in different printing modes at a later date. This is a great advantage that the textile designer has over the serigrapher. Occasionally, serigraphers have attempted to produce a separate frame for each color, but too frequently it is impractical.

The printer can take an additive approach, printing one color, developing a new resist and adding it to the first, and so on until the printing is finished. In both serigraphy and textile printing this seems to be most common. The reverse is the subtractive method, in which successive portions of the screen are blocked out. Of course, the two approaches can be combined.

Portions of a single screen resist can be printed with different colors. This can be accomplished in two different ways. Temporary partitions, consisting of thin pieces of cardboard or wood, can be placed inside the frame with masking tape to divide the printing area (Fig. 7–19). If the run is a long one, they should be sealed with shellac or lacquer. A different color is placed in each section, and smaller squeegees are used, one for each color. When the frame is placed on the printing material, each of the two or three colors is squeegeed, in turn, before the frame is lifted. But although you can print two or three colors at one time, it is difficult to keep each color area rigidly separated by the temporary partitions. (A variation is to place two colors in the frame at the same time without the partition. They will mix together during the printing process and blend. This method demands much more skill to maintain some sort of consistency between the various prints of an edition or the units in a textile pattern. But such consistency need not always be the goal of the artist.) A second method calls for printing a single screen resist with the first color after blocking portions of it with

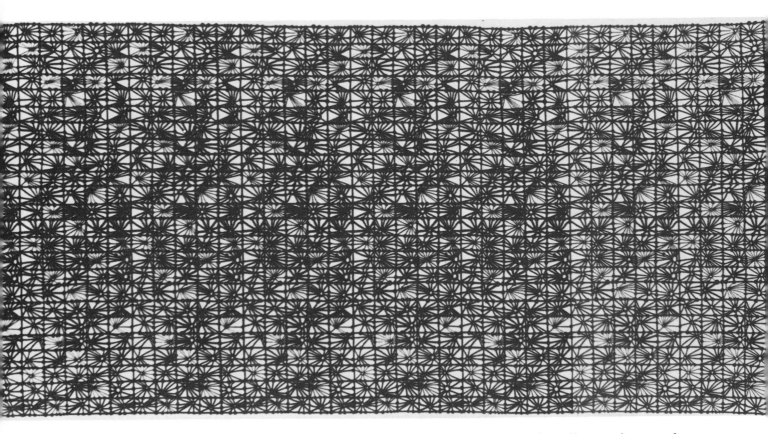

Fig. 7–18.   A light-sensitive emulsion film stencil was used to produce this textile print, entitled "Loge's Tarnhelm." (By Mathilda V. Schwalbach)

Fig. 7–19.   Two colors can be printed at the same time by dividing the screen with a thin wood or stiff cardboard partition and sealing the partition at both ends and along the screen to prevent paint leakage.

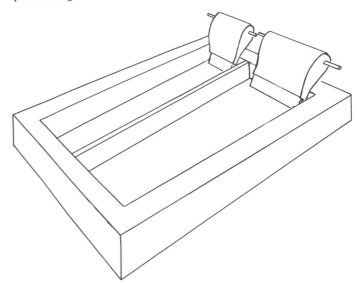

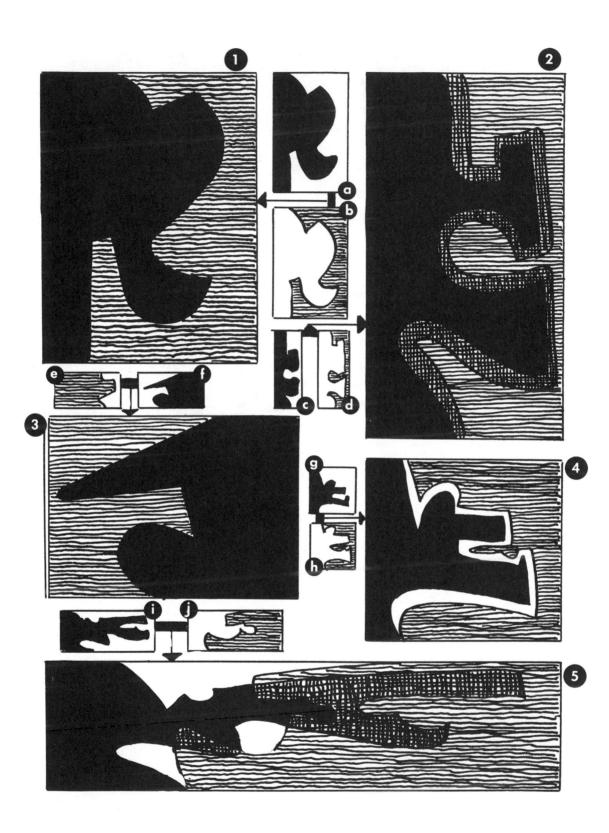

Fig. 7–20. There are five basic ways in which two stencils can be used together in a design: (1) stencils a and b are printed so that their edges fit perfectly together with no overlap or gap between, which is very difficult to accomplish and requires excellent registration techniques; (2) stencils c and d overlap each other slightly, creating the effect of a line between them where the second color, which is transparent, has overprinted the first color; (3) stencils e and f have very different edges and overlap a great deal, but the second color printed is opaque and it completely covers up the edge of the first color; (4) stencils g and h have similar edges and are printed with a gap between, again creating a linear effect but this time with the background color instead of the two colors overlapping; (5) stencils i and j have dissimilar edges that overlap in some places and leave gaps in others, and the second color is a transparent ink, combining the effect produced in (2) and (4).

paper on the underside. Then the second color is printed using the same resist with other portions blocked off with a paper stencil. Colors can be overlapped and mixed as the printer wishes. This can be repeated with the single screen resist as many times as it suits the printer. With two screen resists there are five ways of printing color areas (see Fig. 7–20).

While the serigrapher might be interested in materials other than paper for an expression of his ideas, he has such a wide range of paper surfaces and thicknesses that he has traditionally limited himself pretty much to paper. Some Op and Pop artists have experimented with plastics. But we would suggest that the beginner at least, select a paper that suits him and then work with it. Because quantities of paper can be used even in a single edition, the serigrapher should investigate the possibility of purchasing his paper directly from a wholesale house in 100-sheet or ream quantities.

Because of the many new fabrics on the market, the textile printer has a much more complicated problem. Some fabrics reject some printing media, and it is wise to test the acceptance and fastness of any ink or dye paste on a particular fabric before printing it in any quantity.

Since most fabrics contain sizing, it is important that any fabric be thoroughly washed (machine washed, if possible) before printing. After thorough washing and rinsing, iron the fabric smooth and roll it over a paper tube. Cardboard mailing tubes are excellent, but adequate substitutes can be made with rolls of newsprint. The thorough washing will remove the sizing or stiffening from the fabric, which will then accept the color more successfully. It may be possible to obtain fabrics from one of the suppliers that distribute fabrics for controlled laboratory testing. These fabrics are limited in color (usually white or off-white), but they are unsized and unfinished, which makes them ready for immediate printing. (One of the better-known suppliers is Testfabrics, Inc., P.O. Drawer O, 200 Blackford Avenue, Middlesex, N.J. 08846).

For textile printing, choose basic and conventional cottons, linens, or silks for the best results. Generally avoid fabrics with special finishes or new chemical treatments, which will prevent the fibers from properly absorbing the textile paints, inks, or dye pastes. Try fabrics such as tobacco cloth, muslin, sheeting, piqué, linen, crash, Indian Head broadcloth, voile, dull spun rayon, poplin, percale, osnaburg, nainsook, lawn, denim, chambray, balloon cloth, hoya cloth, hopsacking, pellon, and felt. Purchase ½-yard pieces or use old towels or remnants large enough for experimental printing before investing in quantity. Light colors are best for the first experiments, and middle-value colors can be very interesting; dark colors are very difficult to print.

Some of the more unpredictable fabrics that might be suitable for the average designer-craftsman who wishes to print textiles with *water-based commercial textile paint* are Dacron and cotton poplin with permanent press, polyester (65 per cent) and cotton poplin (35 per cent) with permanent press, Dacron polyester (100 per cent), Arnel triacetate (100 per cent), and nylon chiffon (100 per cent). Acceptable with *Anthrasol dye pastes* are polyester (65 per cent) and cotton poplin (35 per cent) with permanent press, Dacron polyester (100 per cent), Arnel triacetate (100 per cent), Blue C polyester (65 per cent) and cotton broadcloth (35 per cent) with permanent press, acrylic (100 per cent), rayon "linen" weave (100 per cent), nylon chiffon (100 per cent), and rayon (74 per cent) and acetate (26 per cent).

Since many of the printing media are very volatile and dry quickly, check everything carefully before starting to print. It is not easy to stop a printing operation, once begun, to make repairs or take care of something that should have been done earlier. If it is necessary to stop, inks in the printing frame and in the screen mesh can be prevented from drying for a reasonable period of time by placing the printing frame down with the underside on absorbent scrap paper such as old newspapers. Lightly rub the screen with the solvent used with the ink, leaving the screen mesh somewhat saturated. Then place more newspapers over the mesh on the inside of the frame and lightly soak the paper in a similar manner. Normally this cannot be done until most of the ink has been taken out of the frame. If the frame is to sit for only a short period, leave it on a freshly printed image, but watch it carefully for signs of drying. When printing is resumed, print several times on newspaper to clear the passage of ink through the meshes.

Here is a list of checks that can be made just before printing to prevent accidents and delays: (1) Be sure the paint is handy and set where it is not likely to touch the paper or fabric being printed. (2) Inspect the squeegee. Is it clean? Does it cover the printing width? Will it fit inside the screen frame? Are there nails or dowels inserted in each end so it can be placed in the frame without sliding into the printing ink? (3) Do you have clean rags or cleansing tissues handy? A paste cleansing cream is useful for easy, quick cleaning of dirty hands. (Consider using disposable plastic gloves to protect your hands during printing.) (4) Check the screen mesh. Is the design adhered properly? What about pinholes in the screen resist? If undesired, they will need to be filled in with the proper resist material. Is the tape sealing the edges firm and not likely to leak? Look on both the underside and the inside. Are there any damp paint smudges left on the screen (particularly the underside) from the previous color run? (5) In serigraphy, check to see if the hinges, the side register blocks, and the frame locks are tight. Are the register tabs correct? Check by placing one of the prints or the original under the frame in printing position. Lower the frame before the ink has been placed in the frame to check the register. Does the frame meet the printing surface properly, or is the printing paper too thick or too thin? Make adjustments of the frame. (6) In textile printing, check the register by placing the frame in the properly keyed position on the fabric before the paint has been placed in the frame. Check that the screw eyes are set at the proper length. Are all the gauge bolts securely fastened and the proper distance apart? Is the fabric securely fastened to the surface of the printing table? Has the previous color dried sufficiently to accept an overprint? (7) Have you planned for a drying setup when the fabric or serigraph edition is printed? In serigraphy, is the drying place for prints convenient to the printing area? Will it accept the number of prints in the edition?

When everything checks out, the last step in preparation is to wipe the screen mesh lightly on the inside with a clean rag dampened with the solvent being used in the

Fig. 7–21. Some design units are too long for one printer to handle himself, and two must pass the squeegee back and forth to each other. This requires a certain degree of sensitivity and rhythm to pressure variations to produce a good print.

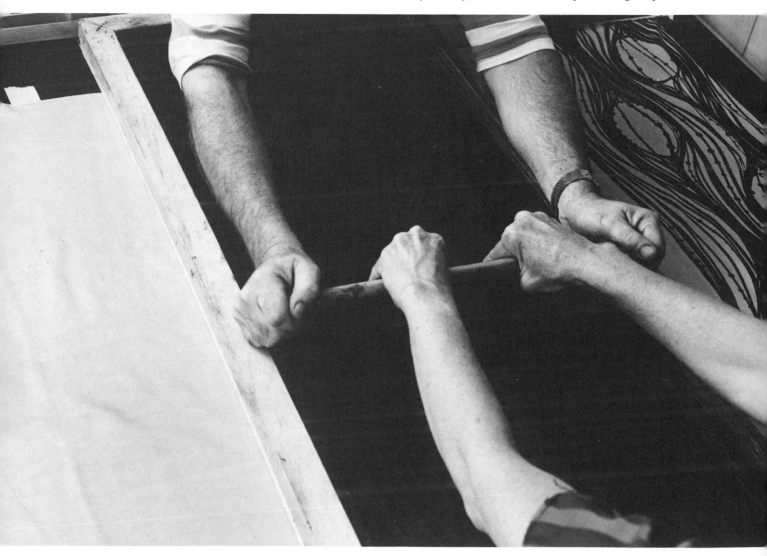

printing medium. This will speed up acceptance of the ink into the meshes of the screen. It also inhibits screen clogging and the staining of the meshes. Replace the screen frame in the proper printing position. Put the squeegee in the frame with the blade between one end of the frame and the edge of the design to be printed to keep the ink from running into the openings of the stencil. Spread a suitable quantity of ink along the entire width of the area to be printed and between the squeegee blade and the end of the frame. You are now ready to print.

In serigraphy, pull the squeegee in *the same direction* each time if you want accurate register. Because there is a slight resilience in mesh fabrics, the screen will print differently depending upon the direction in which the squeegee is pulled. If it is more convenient that you pull the squeegee in both directions, you will need to number your prints in sequence as you print them. All the even-numbered prints can then be printed by pulling the squeegee in one direction and the odd-numbered prints by pulling the squeegee in the opposite direction on each color run. At the end of the squeegee stroke, if you are pulling the squeegee in only one direction, bring the squeegee blade sharply up against the wooden end of the printing frame, scoop up the ink, and carry it back to the opposite end. Printing streaks will be avoided if the ink is kept on one side of the squeegee blade. Keep the other side relatively free of ink. In printing serigraphs, the squeegee is generally held at an angle of 60 degrees.

In printing fabrics, the blade is pulled back and forth or, on wide fabrics, passed between two printers (Fig. 7–21). To keep the ink on only one side of the printing blade, the squeegee can be raised at the end of each stroke and carefully turned around. This must be done slowly or ink will fly off the blade. In textile printing, the best angle for the squeegee is about 45 degrees. This forces more of the ink into the fibers of the cloth. The squeegee may be pulled over the cloth as many as four or five times in each direction. In a serigraph, one pull is usually adequate.

Your first prints should be trial, or proof, prints. Use newsprint or something similar for serigraphs and a piece of cloth similar to the printing fabric for textiles. In serigraphy, five or six proof prints allow the ink to saturate the mesh of the screen properly, give you a chance to sense the pressure and rhythm necessary for successful application of the inks, and let you make final check on the color. Most errors can be eliminated during proof printing.

In textiles, print alternate units to give the ink a chance to dry before you come back for the intervening units. If you are aiming at a texture caused by deliberate pinholing of the resist, you will need to make a number of test prints to stabilize the amount of pinholing you are getting. For this, the viscosity of your ink is critical.

Serigraphers working for impasto effects should use paper stencils on 10XX or 12XX screen meshes or cotton organdy. Some paints will deposit a heavier layer than others, so experimentation with the mixtures is necessary.

Regular screen paint can be thickened with cornstarch if all other methods fail. The squeegee must be pulled slowly and evenly with a minimum of pressure. The texture will vary from print to print, but the shape should not. If your register is excellent, overprinting of the same area after the first layer has dried will build the color even higher. Generally speaking, the thickness of the paint deposited will equal the thickness of the paper or cardboard used in the stencil resist. The underside will need checking, and paint that has smudged outside of the printing areas must be carefully wiped off.

Another technique for depositing a heavy layer of ink or paint is "flooding." The frame is lifted slightly above the printing surface so it does not touch. While it is held up, the squeegee pulls the ink or paint over the image, charging it fully with ink. The frame is then lowered on the printing surface and the squeegee passes over it a second time with the normal printing movement. This will result in a somewhat heavier ink or paint deposit.

For a luminous effect very much like a rubbing, glue various thin materials (such as cloth, burlap, pebbled cardboard, sandpaper) to the surface of the printing board in the desired position underneath the printed image. The printing paper for the edition must be light-weight stock, and transparent ink must be used. Keep pressure on the squeegee very consistent. The result is that the transparency of the color will vary slightly, simulating an impasto. It will be more transparent over the raised parts of the material adhered to the printing board and less transparent over the lower portions.

A list of various problems that might turn up follows, and when the remedy is not obvious, one is suggested in parentheses.

Color runs beyond the edge of a paper stencil. This could be caused by too much pressure on the squeegee blade. The stencil might be torn or the paper getting damp and allowing paint to soak through. The paper stencil has buckled (try carefully cutting a slot in the buckle so it will adhere flatly with a slight overlap; be careful not to cut the screen mesh). The color mixture is too thin. There may be too much space between the screen resist and the printing surface (again, raise the printing surface slightly by placing a thin sheet of paper or cardboard, as large as the area being printed but smaller than the inside area of the printing frame, underneath).

Uneven printing that is not consistently uneven. This could be caused by an imperfect squeegee blade. The color could be unevenly and insufficiently mixed. There are lumps or other unwanted substances in the paint, or the mixture is too thick. There is an insufficient amount of ink in the screen so that you can run out of ink during a pull of the squeegee. The pressure on the squeegee blade is uneven. Lint from cleaning rags or tissues clogs the screen (place a recent print that is not yet dry under the screen and print again. The sticky ink on the print will pull off the lint). In printed textiles, there was insufficient steaming of the dye in textile printing. Moisture from condensation has reached certain parts of the fabric during the steaming process and stained the cloth.

Consistently uneven printing. The printing surface is warped or uneven. There is something under the printing material that causes an uneven clearance between the screen mesh and the paper or fabric being printed. The stencil is too thick. The frame is warped. The printing paper is too thick for the hinged setup of the printing frame (shim up both ends of the printing frame to raise it above the printing board).

Darker lines appearing parallel to the squeegee blade. The blade has vibrated while being pulled or has been pulled at an irregular rate. This sometimes happens when inexperienced printers pass the blade across the printing table in textile printing. It also happens when the squeegee jumps because the screen mesh is too dry and void of paint or when there is a sudden and radical change in the angle of the blade stroke or the pressure applied with the squeegee.

Small specks appear in various parts of the color areas. The screen is clogging because the paint is drying too rapidly. The paper or cloth is too absorbent for the medium used. (In serigraphy, print the paper with a solid area of the transparent-base mixture; cover the entire print, and it will act as a primer coat; after it has dried, print your color on top. In textile printing, make additional pulls of the squeegee.) In a photogelatin stencil, the gelatin was unevenly applied and is breaking down, or it was foamy, or the number of coats was inadequate (if these problems are minor, the pinholes can be covered with glue or lacquer, but in most cases the gelatin stencil will have to be replaced).

Misregistration of the image. The screen resist is inaccurately cut or badly registered. The registration marks have shifted. The hinges have come loose in serigraphy. The T-plate gauge bolts or screw eyes have worked loose in textile printing. The frame was placed on the textile carelessly. The paper was placed in the register tabs carelessly. Too much pressure on the squeegee has caused the screen mesh to ripple. The screen fabric may have come loose. The printing frame in textile printing may have shifted with the pull of the squeegee. The moisture content of the paper has radically changed because of a change in humidity in the studio.

Ink leaking through the sealed edges of the screen. A cut or leak in the screen mesh has developed (it can be temporarily sealed with masking tape and permanently sealed with lacquer or shellac). The protective taping on either the inside or the underside of the frame is torn and needs to be replaced.

Light or dark streaks in the color area being printed. There is a nick in the squeegee blade. There is insufficient ink in the frame. There are lumps or bits of grit in the paint. The paint is not evenly mixed.

Lines or areas do not print in a tusche-and-glue stencil resist. The tusche layer is not heavy enough or the glue mixture is too heavy (try to flick off the glue-covered

tusche with a dull knife or scrub it with a nail brush or a toothbrush, being careful not to damage the fabric of the screen mesh).

The edges of the drawing in a tusche-glue resist are fuzzy and unclear. The screen meshes are too coarse (make a new stencil and try wiping the cornstarch solution suggested in Chapter 6 on the screen mesh before the tusche is applied).

Double printing of the image. In textile printing you are printing a second color over a first color before it has dried sufficiently. (Print alternate units of the design. Place dry newsprint paper over the first printed units when the in-between unit is printed. It may be necessary to wipe the underside of the screen carefully after each impression is printed.)

Blurring of the image. The ink is too thin and is being forced under the screen resist when squeegeed. The squeegee pressure is too great. The squeegee angle is too low. The blade of the squeegee is getting dull. The silk is loose (if not too serious, place a thin piece of paper or cardboard under the printing material). The printing paper may be pressed too tightly against the screen. It should drop off easily when the frame is lifted. If you have to peel it off it tends to blur (a thin cardboard placed under *both* the hinged end and the opposite end of the printing frame will raise it slightly above the printing surface).

Slight discolorations in the fabric to be printed after it has been glued to the board. The glue solution was put on carelessly and too heavily in some spots (in most cases it will disappear when the glue has dried).

The last step in the printing process is the drying of the fabrics or serigraphs. Prints should hang up or stay in a drying rack for at least thirty minutes before another color is run. When you print with paper-stencil resists, the paper stencil will stick to a print that is not completely dry. This is likely to tear or damage the stencil. Prints can be dried in elaborately constructed drying racks set on rollers so they can be moved near the printing area or on one of several hanging devices that can easily be improvised (Figs. 7–22 and 7–24). They do not take

Fig. 7–22. Wooden clothespins can be strung on wire or strong cord (1) for drying wet prints, or they can be attached to the sides of a wooden frame (2) that is placed with one end on a window sill and the other suspended from the top of the window by wire.

Fig. 7–23. In this studio, prints are simply suspended from clothespins hung on a wire to dry.

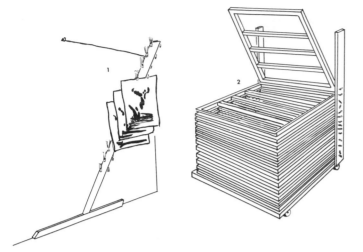

Fig. 7–24. Another drying device is a T-shaped one made of 1-by-2-inch lumber (1). The horizontal part of the T fits into the corner where the floor and wall meet, and the vertical part, which has clothespins attached to hold prints, is suspended away from the wall with wire. This rack can be easily stored when not in use. The professional drying rack at right (2) is quite large. Each shelf, which holds prints flat, is hinged at the back, and the rack is on rollers so that it can be moved close to the printing area.

up too much room and are easily stored. If the prints are on stiff cardboard, they can be placed in a rack designed for phonograph records or a similar rack that can easily be constructed from coat-hanger wire. To test whether a print is dry, touch it lightly with your finger. If it is sticky, it is still too wet. If not sticky, rub or pull the finger lightly over the surface of the print. If it is dry, the finger will move easily and smoothly. If it is still damp, there will be a slight pull on the finger. Be very careful in touching the surface of the print because most inks are very sensitive to scratches and abrasions.

Drying printed textiles requires some forethought. They can be dried on the printing board, of course. However, when the printing surface is needed for successive printing, you must be able to move quickly and easily. Wall surfaces or bulletin boards to which the wet print can be tacked or taped take care of some lengths. Laundry drying racks or laundry lines may be easily reached. In good weather a light breeze assists quick drying. Lines or wires strung up even temporarily are helpful. In professional environments, where production is voluminous and constant, overhead racks and structures are generally constructed exclusively for drying purposes. Poles or pulleys lift the fabric to its drying position. Blowers or fans may be used to aid the drying process. The beginning of a piece can then be drying while another section of it is still being printed below.

Naturally, care must be taken in carrying or shifting wet printed fabrics. Any drying surface or space may be spotted and smeared by the wet fabrics. Wipe up any stains or spots before they dry. Do not fold fabrics while they are still damp.

Pigments in oil emulsion have volatile components that must be removed from fabrics printed with them. This is usually accomplished by heat setting, but if the fabric is not washed for a six-month period, the volatile parts of the ink will evaporate naturally and heat setting will be unnecessary.

Commercially produced water-based textile paints must be heat-set. Ironing for five minutes at the proper setting for the fabric is recommended; repeat on the reverse side. But allowing the print to age after heat setting is also beneficial. Best results are obtained if the fabric is not washed until several weeks have elapsed. You will notice that excess pigment disappears from the surface of the fabric, resulting in a slight color change, and you should anticipate this when mixing the colors for printing. All hand-printed fabrics deserve special care in laundering. Wash the fabric gently as you would fine lingerie and avoid rubbing the printed portions. Hand-printed textiles can also be dry-cleaned.

Textiles printed with Indigosol or fiber-reactive dye pastes are heat-set in a steam box (Fig. 7–25), and the colors are quite permanent. Protect the printed piece by laying it on a long sheet of clean paper (white newsprint or wrapping paper) and rolling it up in the manner of a jelly roll. Be sure that the paper is wider and longer than the fabric so that it will completely protect it. Place the roll in a steam box on a rack above the boiling water. Protect it from condensation inside of the box with layers of newsprint and felt both below and above the roll. Any drops of condensed water that reach the fabric will stain it. Nothing should touch the sides of the steam box. The fabric is steamed for 10 to 15 minutes, taken out, unrolled, and re-rolled in the opposite direction. The steaming process is then repeated for another 10 to 15 minutes. These times are only approximate. The tightness of the roll, the weight of the fabric, and the type of dye used will dictate the steaming time needed. It is wise to experiment with the textiles you are using. When the fabric is removed, *immediately unroll it* and hang it up to dry. A steam iron may also be used to heat-set the fabric. This is mechanically easier, but the fumes generated by the steam ironing are obnoxious. Be sure the room is well ventilated. After drying from the steaming process, aging of the fabric for three days is recommended. Washing in sudsy water then removes the excess dye paste, but in this process the textile must be worked and rinsed until the water runs clear.

Fig. 7–25. A metal steamer for steaming dye pastes can be built and used quite easily. The box should be about 1 foot longer on each end than the standard width of fabric that you expect to print. The diagram shows the setup: cover of galvanized metal (A); felt padding to absorb condensation (B); folded newsprint, also to absorb condensation (C); wrapped roll of printed cloth to be steamed (D); folded newsprint (E); felt padding (F); galvanized steaming box (G); holes to release steam pressure (H); brackets to hold the fabric away from the water (I); water (J); two-burner hot plate (K). The cloth must be carefully rolled in newsprint or other clean paper so that no part of it touches any other part; the paper must be wider than the fabric so that the ends of the roll are protected from water; and the roll must be loosely tied.

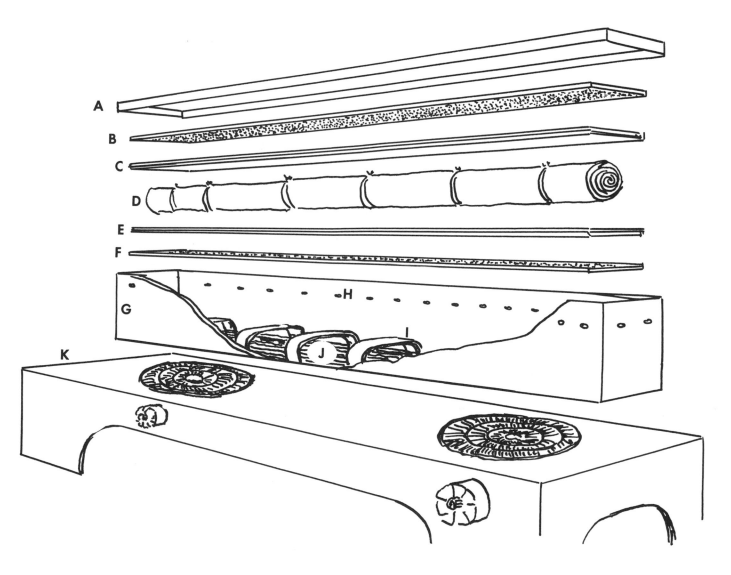

115

Fig. 8–1. Shown in this drawing are a suggested arrangement of studio space for a serigraphic workshop (1) and a detail (2) of the cleaning area. The studio has the following features: designing and drawing area (A); drying area (B); printing area (C); area for mixing inks and paints (D); cleaning area (E); darkroom area (F); light box for exposing light-sensitive emulsions (G); sink for washing and developing light-sensitive emulsions (H); storage (I); ventilator fans (J); light trap for easy entry into the darkroom (K); window (L); work area for enlarger (M); metal cleaning box for cleaning inks from screen frames (N)— the bottom of the box catches and holds paint thinner so that it can easily be washed over the screen; metal-lined fireproof cabinet for combustible paints and cleaners (O); water mixing faucet, with temperature control if possible (P); water hose with spray pressure nozzle (Q); Formica support slanted into the sink to facilitate flow-off of water in cleaning screens (R); sink about 8 inches deep and large enough to handle the largest frames to be used (S); storage cabinet for noncombustible cleaning materials (T); Formica sink top (U).

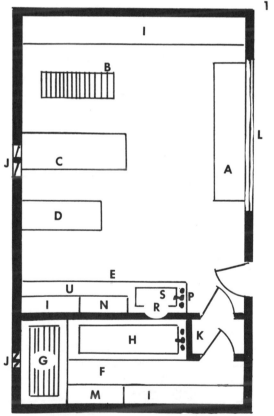

8. CLEANING UP— UNAVOIDABLE AND MESSY

While screen-process equipment does not represent a huge investment for most small printers, its future effectiveness can be seriously diminished if it is not kept in good clean condition. Frames, squeegees, and particularly screen meshes can become relatively difficult to use if they are carelessly or badly cleaned. Paints, inks, or dyes should *never* be left in the screen frame unprotected for even the briefest period. Even if temporary protective measures have been taken, the equipment should be cleaned within a half-hour or less after using. Not only are cleanliness and care necessary for full use of the equipment and materials, but the printer's attitude in these matters will influence the quality of his craftsmanship in the production of his work. Outstanding or even good work rarely comes from a slovenly or careless craftsman.

The Cleaning Area

Cleaning problems can be minimized if some area in the studio or workshop is set aside exculsively for cleaning purposes. You will need a large table for removing the printing media (paints, inks, or dye pastes). Since many different solvents are used, a Formica or acid-proof top is suggested. There should be a metal-lined cabinet for the storage of volatile solvents and a good exhaust fan to pull out the noxious fumes given off by some solvents and paints. Almost all of the paints and solvents have annoying fumes even when they are not hazardous. There should be several metal-covered waste cans for paint- and solvent-soaked materials. Covers that are opened by a foot lever are convenient. Most critical of all, the cleaning

area should be separated from the drawing and designing table and the printing area, and it should not be near the storage-and-handling area for prints, printing paper, and fabrics. The cleaning area can also be used for storing and mixing paints, inks, dyes, and other chemicals. The workshop should have a rather large but not too deep sink that is big enough to handle the maximum frame size you anticipate using. The water (both hot and cold) should come out of a mixing faucet set to one side of the sink. A temperature control on the water mix is not essential, but it would make the stages of the photogelatin resist process that need broad temperature control a good deal easier. A Formica-covered board should be placed on the wall behind the sink with the bottom slanting out so that it overlaps the sink area. Frames to be cleaned can then rest in the sink and lean against the Formica back. This gives an excellent cleaning surface, and all the water and liquids will run directly into the sink. What we are suggesting is, of course, the best possible studio setup (Fig. 8–1). You probably will not match it, but try to come as close as your finances allow.

While old rags are invaluable for cleaning, they are often hard to come by and relatively expensive. Paper tissues of various types are often so heavily used that the serious printer should consider buying them by the case. Some clean rags should be kept to wipe the screen while printing because paper tissues, particularly the softer ones, tend to leave lint. A rubber spatula is an excellent device to scoop out extra paint from the frame after printing. Small bits of old stiff cardboard are helpful also in scraping off paint and other paste materials—a good use for old mat board.

Personal cleanliness is as important as clean materials,

Fig. 8–2. The techniques of screen printing and free painting were combined to produce these textile prints. (By Irene Naik)

room, and equipment. The mark of the careless craftsman is usually found on his work. Poor color mixtures, stains, paint smears, and finger marks on prints and fabrics are aesthetically inexcusable. As we suggested earlier, two printers working at one time make the operation a little easier and smoother. Some staining and dirt on the hands of the printer is unavoidable, however, and if you must work alone, stop frequently to check cleanliness both of yourself and the operation. Tissues and cleansing creams should be kept next to you where you can use them at any moment. Protecting your hands before printing with a cream makes cleaning much easier. People who have problems with skin irritations should use disposable plastic gloves. Heavy rubber gloves are a necessity for working with some of the strong chemicals used in the production and removal of screen resists, and a good heavy rubber apron is an excellent protector. Plenty of old newspapers should be stacked in the workroom.

Some care needs to be taken in the cleaning procedures. Most screen meshes are extremely tough and with proper handling are able to sustain a great deal of punishment. However, never scrub on a screen without supporting it so that no excessive pressure or friction is placed on the mesh. When scrubbing the inside of the mesh, place it against a smooth surface. When scrubbing the underside, put the frame on its side and simultaneously rub from both the inside and the underside of the screen. Thus, no pressure is placed on the screen mesh, and yet the screen mesh gets a thorough scrubbing.

Cleaning Solvents

One always hopes that some day there will be a universal cleaner or solvent. The materials used in the screen process are so varied that the problem of which solvent and which cleaner to use can get complicated. When several different materials are used in the screen resist, two or three different solvents might be needed to remove it. And still another solvent might be needed to clean off the printing medium. Some materials can be left on the screen for indefinite periods of time; others must be removed after a short time or the screen will be permanently damaged. The screen mesh may be the most expensive part of screen-printing equipment, but if given good care it can last for a surprising number of printing projects.

Special paints and materials should, in most cases, be thinned and washed off the screen with the special thinners and washup designed by the manufacturer to work best with the special product you are using. The materials listed below are fairly common, readily available solvents and cleaners.

Material to be dissolved	Solvents
Asphaltum (dry)	Gasoline
Dye pastes (dry)	Warm or cold sudsy water
Enamel paint (wet)	Kerosene, mineral spirits, oleum, paint thinner, turpentine
Finger paint	Water
Light-hardened photogelatin	Equal parts household bleach and water. Follow manufacturer's suggestions with commercial gelatins. An enzyme digester also works with many photogelatin screens
Hide glue (dry)	Hot water
Grease on screen mesh	Trisodium phosphate
Gum arabic or gum tragacanth	Warm water
Hardened paint	Acetone, lacquer thinner, liquid brush cleaner, butyl acetate
Lacquer (oil)	Mineral spirits
Lacquer (cellulose)	Lacquer thinner, lacquer-film solvent, butyl acetate, acetone
Lacquer film	Lacquer thinner, lacquer-film solvent, butyl acetate, acetone
Lithographic crayon	Kerosene, turpentine, paint thinner, oleum, mineral spirits
Lithographic tusche (wet)	Water
Lithographic tusche (dry)	Kerosene, turpentine, paint thinner, oleum, mineral spirits
Maskoid	Rub off
Oil screen-process inks	Kerosene, mineral spirits, paint thinner, oleum, turpentine
Rubber cement	Rub off, rubber-cement thinner, benzene, xylol
Shellac	Alcohol
Stains on nylon screen	Household bleach (do not use on silk mesh)
Tempera paint (water)	Water
Textile paint (water-based)	Warm or cold water
Textile paint (oil-based)	Mineral spirits, paint thinner, oleum, turpentine, kerosene
Water-soluble blockout	Water
Wax crayon	Mineral spirits, paint thinner, oleum, turpentine, kerosene
Wax paraffin	Heat with iron on absorbent paper, naptha, commercial dry-cleaning fluid

Screen painting can be a very pleasurable and rewarding experience, but it can also result in tragedy. Serious burns, toxic skin conditions, internal damage to the respiratory system, explosions, and fires can result from ignorant and careless practices. All work should be done in well-ventilated areas. This usually means more than just opening a window. If a great deal of printing is done, the

workroom should have adequate exhaust fans. Many of the chemicals and paints should be stored in fireproof metal cabinets. If possible, these cabinets should be locked so that children and uninformed persons cannot get into them. In inflammable materials, it is usually the fumes that burn and not the liquid. Open flames, motors that cause sparking, large electric lightbulbs, or anything that might cause accumulated fumes to explode should not be used or placed in the workshop area. Since most of the fumes are heavier than air, the exhaust should be as near floor level as practical. Some solvents such as acetone, gasoline, and xylol are highly inflammable. Others like carbon tetrachloride and benzene are extremely toxic. *Before you use any solvents unfamiliar to you, carefully observe the manufacturer's directions; they are usually printed on the container.* Cleaning rags should be hung

in a ventilated space until dry, and waste papers and rags stored in fireproof metal containers until they can be burned or safely discarded. In mixing chemicals, always add the chemical to the water in small amounts. *Never add water to the chemical.* Chemical reaction can cause eruptions and explosions. Textile printers using a steam box should be very careful of the hot steam imprisoned in it. Open and close the box with insulated gloves for protection against metal and steam burns.

Cleaning a New Screen

Even a new silk-screen mesh needs to be cleaned. After the screen mesh has been stretched but before it has been taped, clean it with a detergent. Then rinse the screen and sprinkle trisodium phosphate over the wet mesh, working it with a soft nylon scrubbing brush. It is good practice to have a separate brush or sponge for each cleaning operation. Label each so you can keep them separate. Rinse the screen again with clean water. Then brush over the screen with a sponge or rag saturated with a 5 per cent acetic acid solution (vinegar can be used). Rinse the screen thoroughly with water to remove the solution from the screen mesh. This cleaning process will not only prepare the new frame for printing but will shrink the screen mesh slightly and tighten it further.

Nylon meshes should be similarly cleaned. However, the smooth finish of nylon mesh requires a slight roughening of the fibers on new screens. This produces a "tooth" on the fiber that helps adhere the screen resist. It is particularly helpful for photogelatin-emulsion resists. To produce this tooth, rub the screen with pumice or one of the less gritty household scouring powders in place of the detergent used first on the silk mesh. Then follow through with the same cleaning procedure used with a new silk mesh.

Since nylon mesh is not affected by strong cleaners as is silk mesh, some printers use a 20 per cent caustic soda (sodium hydroxide) solution on both sides as the first step in cleaning a new nylon screen before it is taped. This can be made by adding one heaping teaspoon of lye to one pint of water. Leave the solution on a new screen for fifteen to twenty minutes; on a used screen the time is reduced to ten minutes. Wear rubber or plastic gloves and take care not to splash the liquid into your eyes. After the soaking period, rinse the screen in water. If the screen is new, sprinkle pumice or a fine household scouring powder that contains an active alkaline degreasing agent on the screen and rub it into the mesh with a second nylon brush or sponge. The fine meshes of nylon cannot be scrubbed as hard as the coarser ones. Then wash the fabric again thoroughly with water. Now rub the screen down with the 5 per cent acetic acid solution (or vinegar) and a third nylon brush or sponge to neutralize the alkalines used previously. Then rinse again thoroughly with cold water.

Cleaning Off the Printing Medium

There are two cleaning processes that a printer must go through each time he prints a color run. The first is the removal of the printing medium (the paints, inks, or dye pastes). This is always necessary. The second process, removing the screen resist from the screen mesh, is necessary only when the next color run is going to require a new screen resist.

For removal of an oil-based medium, immediately after printing unhinge the printing frame and carry it to the cleaning area.

Place the printing frame on the cleaning surface over a thick pad of old newspaper. With a rubber spatula, scoop the unused ink from the screen frame into a small metal can. Small soup and beverage cans are ideal for this. With the mixing stick, apply a thin layer of wet paint around the outside of the very top of the can. Scrape the rest of the paint down inside the can, and level the surface by tapping the can down *lightly* on the table to settle the paint. Pour a thin layer of paint thinner, turpentine, or mineral spirits into the can to retard the formation of a hard coating on the surface. Carefully cover the top of the can with a double thickness of kitchen wrapping plastic. Press the plastic around the outside edge of the can into the thin layer of wet paint. Seal with a rubber band around the top edge of the can. The paint under the plastic will harden and make a very effective seal; the plastic will allow you to look at the color without breaking this seal. (An additional suggestion is to note on a piece of masking tape stuck to the outside of the can the composition of the mixture and its transparency.) Paints stored in this way will keep for very long periods.

After all of the paint has been scooped out of the printing frame, rub the inside with dry newspapers or paper towels. Pour into the frame plenty of the proper solvent so that any traces of paint become liquid. Rub the solvent into the mesh with a rag or paper towels. The solvent should literally flow around the inside of the frame while you rub it hard against the newspaper. If you are a prolific printer, it will pay to construct a metal cleaning box.

Lift up the screen frame and wipe off the excess solvent with a dry rag or paper towels. Tear away the top one or two layers from the pad of newspaper under the screen. Repeat this process as many times as necessary to clear the meshes of the screen completely and to remove all traces of paint from the frame. If some areas seem to be stubborn and resist cleaning, hold the screen vertically and rub simultaneously from both sides with rags or paper towels soaked in the solvent.

After the screen is clean, use the same solvent to clean the squeegee. Pay particular attention to the place where the squeegee blade is attached to the handle. Clean the rubber spatula, mixing sticks, palette knives, and anything else that has come in contact with the printing medium. Deposit all of the solvent-soaked rags and papers in a covered metal can or burn them immediately in a trash burner. Rags that cannot be safely disposed of immediately should be hung so that they air-dry thoroughly.

Cleaning out non-oil-based printing mediums calls for exactly the same procedure except that a different solvent may be used. Follow the directions of the manufacturer of the equipment. Leftover water-based printing paint can be stored in a covered container, but dye pastes should be discarded since they deteriorate. In an emergency they can be kept refrigerated for a few days, but it

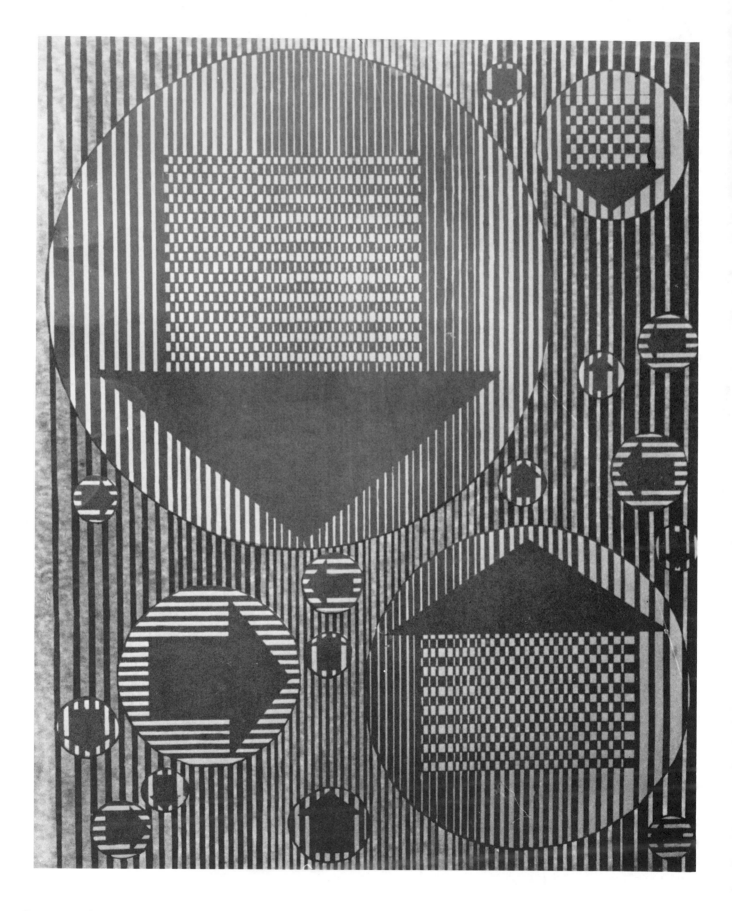

Fig. 8–4. "This-a-way That-a-way" takes its inspiration from some of the techniques of Op art. (Serigraph, by James A. Schwalbach)

is not recommended. After the printing medium has been removed, take the screen to the sink and spray it thoroughly with warm water. If you have a photogelatin resist on the screen that you wish to save, wash cautiously with cool water to protect the resist from disintegrating (especially if it has not been hardened). If it is a nylon screen, the color can be wiped (without rinsing) from the inside surface with soft paper cleansing tissues. When cleaned in this manner, subsequent printing should involve a color related to the previous run since any color left on the stencil will blend into the next color run. For example, if red has been used, a red-violet or red-orange should follow, since a reddish touch from the first run will be evident in the new color run as well. This system of chain color printing can lead to unusual effects and nuances.

Removing the Screen Resist

Now that the printing medium has been cleaned off the screen and the meshes are clear, the next step is to remove the screen resist if you have no further need for it. All screen resists except paper and glue can be kept on the screen almost indefinitely after cleaning. This is not normal practice for serigraphers since the screen is usually needed for the next screen resist, but textile designers often save screen frames used in a fabric pattern so that they can duplicate the fabric print in the same color scheme or a new one. New variations of the pattern printing sequence and arrangement can be devised at a future date.

A paper resist is usually removed immediately after the unused printing medium has been scooped out of the frame and before the frame has been cleaned, and then is discarded. Generally it gets damaged in this process, but with considerable luck a printer might be able to get the paper stencil off in one piece. It should then be carefully wiped with a clean rag and stored between two sheets of wax paper protected between two pieces of heavy cardboard. This, however, is unusual.

Any screen resist using glue may be stored for a few days, but it should not be allowed to stand on the screen longer. During the printing process, small bits of the paint and base seep down into crevices in the glue. If allowed to harden, they are extremely difficult to remove from the screen mesh at a later date. Frequently they have the same appearance as the glue resist. Saving a glue resist is even more inadvisable if successive coats of glue have been applied over each other during the printing process. The subsequent glue coatings harden the small bits of paint further.

Glue-resist stencils are very easy to remove. After the printing medium has been cleaned off, set the frame in a large sink and wash or spray it with a warm-water rinse. Light scrubbing with sudsy water also helps to remove any small amounts of the print medium that remain in the screen mesh and speeds up the removal of the glue. Stubborn areas can be loosened by soaking in warm water for a short period of time. After the glue has been removed, clean the frame lightly with the same solvent used for the printing medium. This will take away some of the printing stain and any printing medium that might have been missed earlier. If any stubborn specks of paint remain, use one of the stronger solvents or liquid brush cleaner. Sometimes a hard, fine pressure spray will force out these hardened paint specks.

Stains from a previous printing really do not harm the screen as long as the meshes are open. However, if the stains are highly visible, they might be a seriously distracting element in designing a new image, particularly if you do a good deal of your designing directly on the screen mesh. With careful handling because they are strong, such solvents as acetone or liquid brush cleaner will reduce the visibility of the stain. If the stain is on a nylon screen, a 50 per cent solution of laundry bleach can be used, but if the stain is on a silk screen, the solution of laundry bleach should be reduced to 5 per cent. Apply the 5 per cent bleach solution to the fabric and then rub with a light bristle brush and household cleanser. Use this only on stains that are definitely bothersome, because it will weaken the silk fabric and reduce its life.

After the resist has been removed, all screens should be given the following final cleaning before they are again used or stored: (1) clean with detergent; (2) rinse with clean cold water; (3) clean with trisodium phosphate; (4) rinse with clean cold water; (5) rub with a 5 per cent solution of acetic acid (or vinegar); (6) rinse with cold water; (7) dry thoroughly; (8) check tapes around the inside and bottom side of the frame to be sure that they are in excellent condition. Occasionally recoat them with shellac or clear lacquer.

If your screen resist is made of lacquer (lacquer blockout or cut-film lacquer), place it flat on a thick pad of old newspapers after the screen meshes are clear of the printing medium. Soak the inside of the screen mesh liberally with either lacquer thinner or the manufacturer's recommended film adherent. Scrub it lightly with a similarly soaked rag or paper towels. Allow the frame to soak for a minute or less. Pick up the frame and peel off the layer of old newspapers that adheres to the underside of the screen. Most of the lacquer resist usually soaks into the old newspaper. If an appreciable amount of lacquer resist still remains in the screen, repeat the procedure. When most of it has been removed, hold the screen vertically and rub the screen lightly with solvent-soaked rags or paper simultaneously from both sides. Some printers like to leave one of these rubbing wads dry to pick up the dissolved resist. If there are stubborn bits of lacquer resist that still remain in the screen mesh, use acetone or butyl acetate. *All* of the solvents for lacquer are somewhat noxious and should be used only in an area ventilated by more than just an open window. The acetone and butyl acetate are dangerous so *they must be used outdoors or*

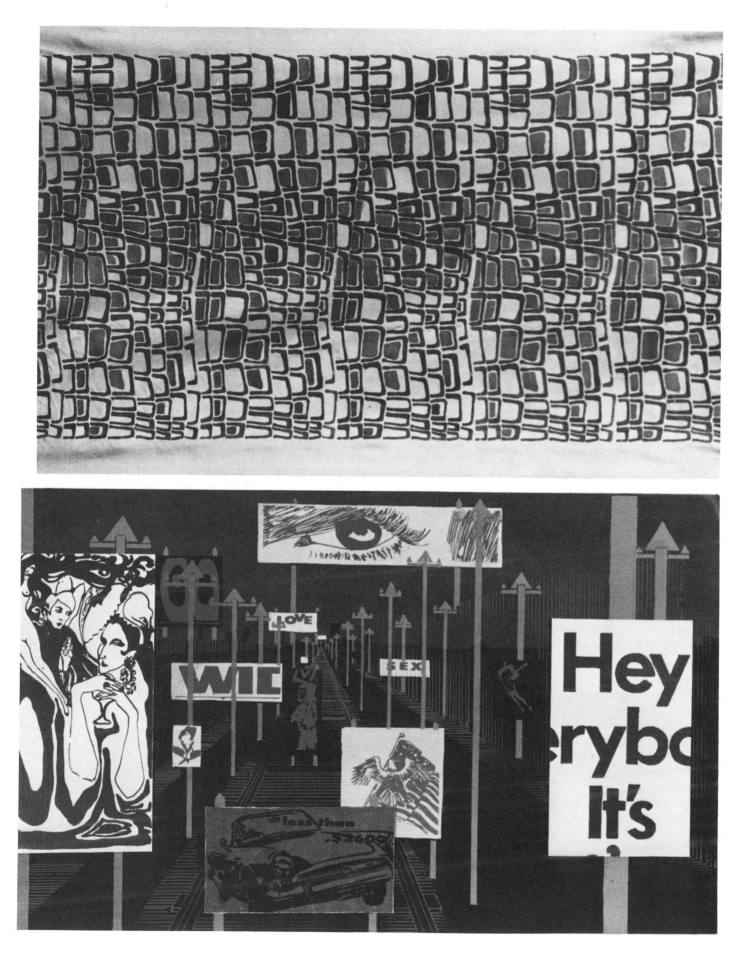

directly behind a fan that constantly carries the air out of the room through a vent or open window. Again, it is a good precaution to rub the screen mesh lightly with the solvent used for the printing medium. This will remove any paint still in the screen mesh. Stubborn and hardened bits of paint can be removed with the acetone, butyl acetate, or liquid brush cleaner. Before using or storing the recently cleaned screen, follow the cleaning and inspection steps given on page 123.

Any of the many other screen resists *except a photo-gelatin emulsion* are cleaned in exactly the same manner as lacquer resists except that the solvent produced for the particular screen-resist substance is used.

Water-soluble commercial blockouts are also removed with warm water, exactly as was the glue blockout. Liquid wax and paraffin wax are removed by applying a hot iron to the mesh over absorbent paper. Final traces of the wax come out with naphtha or dry-cleaning fluid. Stove enamel and asphaltum varnish are removed with gasoline. Masking tape and decals leave very little residue in the screen mesh, which usually can be removed with mineral spirits, lacquer thinner, or dry-cleaning fluid.

Removing a photogelatin-emulsion resist often presents a more difficult and complicated problem. Like cleaning all the other screens, a photogelatin resist must first be thoroughly cleaned to remove the printing medium. Some of the photo emulsions or photosensitive films available through the screen-process supply houses are removed with a hard, fine pressure spray of hot water (120 to 140 degrees) from either special hose nozzles that are available for the purpose or a rubber shower spray. For photogelatin resists that cannot be removed with a hot-water spray, screen-process suppliers market an organic enzyme digester that sets up a chemical action which digests the emulsion without harming the silk mesh. These are nontoxic and fairly easy to use. Follow the directions on the container.

If you are working with a nylon screen mesh, then photo-emulsion resists that cannot be sprayed out with a pressurized stream of hot water can be removed with a 50 per cent solution of household bleach. But do not use this on the silk because it will destroy the fibers. If a hardener of shellac or lacquer has been applied to one or both sides of the screen mesh, it must first be dissolved with the proper solvent before either the hot-water spray, enzyme digester, or household bleach can be effective. If a commercial hardener is used, check with the manufacturer to see if it is possible to remove the hardener. For example, photogelatin resists that have been hardened with caustic resist enamel cannot be removed practically or easily from the screen mesh (polyvinyl alcohol and some commercial emulsions). Check your formula or the manufacturer before using the emulsion.

After the photosensitive emulsion has been removed from the screen, rub it lightly with the solvent used for the printing medium, removing any of the printing medium that might still be in the meshes. Before using or storing the screen, follow the cleaning and inspection procedure given on page 123.

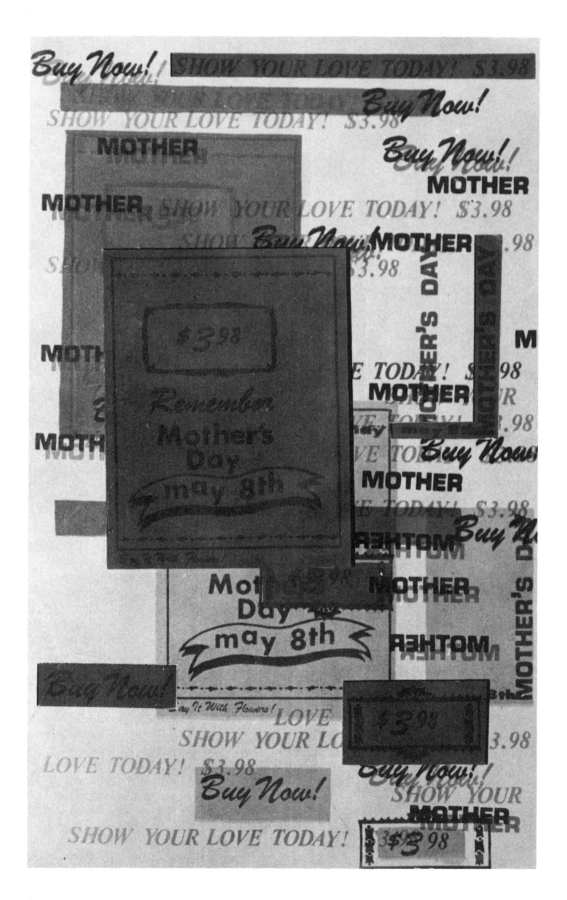

Fig. 9–1. A traditional theme gets a nontraditional treatment in this serigraph.
("Mother's Day," by James A. Schwalbach)

9. HANDLING THE COMPLETED PRINT

An artist should always be proud of what he has produced. To create is not to re-create. To produce serigraphs and printed textiles as personal therapy is not to be condemned or prevented, but it is not the goal of one who would be an artist. An artist must take a few yards of woven fabric or a piece of paper, both more or less ordinary, and make them extraordinary. At least that is what should happen. A bit of the artist's dreams, hopes, sensitivities, glories, and even angers will become a part of the work. The serigraph or printed textile is born anew from the creative womb of the artist. They exist. They are blood kin to the artist. While he should be proud of what he has done, the artist must beware of too much self-satisfaction. To grow and improve continually in a creative field he has to have that nagging feeling that each work produced, somehow, in some way, could have been improved.

The artist, to maintain his individuality, responds sensitively and in a very personal way to his environment and his culture. He needs a certain amount of ego and strength to do this. For, in a way, the artist is "the conscience of mankind." Great works of art are indeed rare and most of us will never produce one, but there is always that chance. But the chance will exist only so long as each work is an earnest, vital, and sensitive response on the part of the artist. These preconditions are the requisites for that rare, magical alchemy that gives greatness to any work of art.

Evaluating Your Work

Self-evaluation is most difficult. Yet it is the evaluation that is most meaningful. Honest evaluation from friends is hard to come by. Evaluation from a dedicated and experienced teacher or fellow artist can help clear one's eyes. The main difficulty in self-evaluation is that one is so close to the work—so many plans and dreams have become part of it and there have been so many trials and retrials—that one is not always sure where he has failed or succeeded. It helps sometimes to let a work age. You will always see things better if you can stand back a few feet. Often it helps to place a work in a public exhibition with other works. This becomes a sort of testing ground. But even here it is the artist who must apply the final test. He must decide how a work holds up in view of his own goals.

The textile designer can find satisfaction in the printed textile in many implicit ways. The combined color, movement, and rhythmic arrangement—or the unexpected joy of the pattern—may reveal itself only after some study of the finished product; well after the in-process struggles and adjustments. It is a juxtapositioning of the difficult with the simple. It is a determined push into the unknown. It is a constant battle with the forces of conformity to make the plain rich, the dull exciting—a feast to the beholder.

Pieces that fall short of these high goals may be con-

Fig. 9–2. Value differences in color can alter the effect of one design considerably. ("Sunburst," by Susan Palm)

sidered at least as a step along the way. One should learn from both successes and failures. If it really disappoints, the textile designer always has the practical option of washing out the design before the final heat setting. The weak image remaining in the fabric may generate a fresh idea that could be overprinted.

The serious serigrapher must face the "selection of the edition." Each will devise his own method, but all the prints must be carefully scrutinized. Any that differs greatly from the rest must be set aside along with any prints with faults (smudges in the margins, bad registration, smearing, streaks). These are to be rejected from the edition. What is left is a nearly identical series of prints. They are not exactly alike. An experienced printer may have 5 to 10 per cent rejections from the original group.

Identification of Work and Keeping Records

For the professional printmaker, the finished edition can be important as a source of income, but even if not primarily concerned with the sale of his work, the printmaker is fairly prolific if he is serious. This suggests that there ought to be some system of identifying works and keeping records. The prints finally selected in an edition are usually signed by the artist in the bottom right-hand margin. In the bottom left-hand margin the print is titled and given an identification number. (In etching and lithography, the number indicates the order in which the prints come off the press, but that has no significance in serigraphy.) For example, 6/35 written after the title indicates that the identifying number for this particular print is 6 and the number of prints in the entire edition is 35. The date can follow this number or it can follow the artist's signature. Some printmakers place the title in the center of the bottom margin; others put the identifying number in the center. There is no one way to do it, but all prints in an edition should contain that information. Rejected prints or proof prints (the first prints made while you are experimenting with the color run) are signed in a similar manner but are labeled "artist's proof." Prints that are not suitable are destroyed.

Professional textile designers sign their work in a similar fashion, but as part of the printing process. Along one edge of the yardage the artist's name is screened and sometimes the title of the design, date of production, and the name and location of the studio. Usually this information is put on acetate and a photogelatin-emulsion resist produced, which is placed on a small screen specially built for this purpose. It is then squeegeed close to one of of the edges approximately every yard. It should not be conspicuous if the textile is to serve as a wall hanging and will probably end up in a hem or seam if the textile finds a practical use. But it serves the same purpose as the signature of the serigrapher: it is testimony to the quality and originality of the work and is useful for the designer in keeping records of his work.

Serigraphs are easily transported, sold, borrowed, and exhibited, and in recent years there has been a growing interest in the exhibition and sale of hand-printed textiles. Because of income-tax considerations and the need to keep track of where a work is at a particular time, it is necessary to keep some simple records. Some printmakers and designers find a card-file index suitable, devoting a card to each edition, on which is recorded the name of the print, its insurance value, retail price, and date of production. The number of prints in the edition and the cost in materials and time are items useful in figuring the annual income-tax report. Sales, loans, and exhibitions can also be recorded on the same card. If the card is quite small, a separate card can be devoted to each print in the edition. Other printmakers find it simpler to keep records in a standard business ledger. Textile designers can keep the same type of records under the title given to each fabric design. When screens are stored for subsequent production, they are labeled with the title of the design.

Matting and Framing a Print

Often a designer does not really see his print until it appears for the first time in a mat, which serves to separate the print from the competing environment. Many printers keep a spare mat handy so that each color run of an edition can be properly viewed for evaluating the results. The mat is usually a smooth or slightly pebbled sheet of heavy white cardboard called mat board. Occasionally a printmaker will use a light cream or gray mat, but strong mat colors tend to compete with the print. Many exhibitions and the National Serigraph Society suggest that mats be cut in one of three sizes: 15 by 20 inches, 20 by 24 inches, or 22 by 28 inches. Because of the difficulty of hanging and shipping, some exhibitions will not accept mats much larger than those sizes.

While cutting a good mat may seem to be a rather simple procedure, there is a great deal of skill involved. If you plan to mat only a few prints, it is better to have your mats cut by someone with experience. Generally, the width of the center hole is ½ inch wider than the width of the print. The height of the hole is ¾ inch higher. This allows the print to be exposed ¼ inch on both sides and the top and ½ inch on the bottom for signing and identifying the print. If the print is matted without such margins, it is signed, dated, and numbered on its surface in the lower right-hand corner; then the title is put on the mat. However, this is not the normal procedure. The side widths of the mat are the same. The size of the mat board may not permit the top width to be the same as the sides. The bottom width is usually wider than the sides and the top. This gives the print a little better optical centering and makes it more comfortable to view (Fig. 9–3). The area of the mat should be sufficient to set off the print from its surroundings.

Cutting the hole requires skill. A good sharp, sturdy mat knife is a necessity, and so is a strong metal straight-

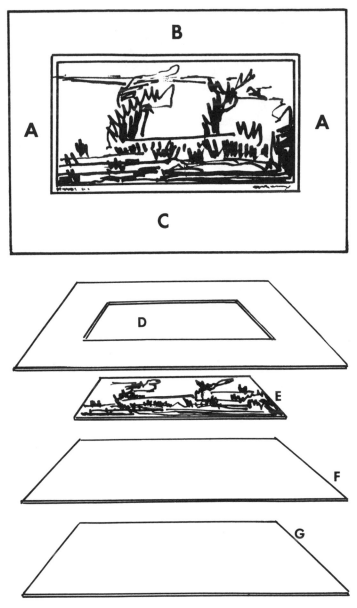

Fig. 9–3. When a print is matted, the sides (A) of the mat are almost always equal in width; the top (B) is frequently the same width but can be slightly larger or smaller; and the bottom (C) is always larger than the top or sides. The hole in the mat (D) should be slightly larger than the print (E). The mat covers the print, which is in turn backed by background paper (F)—a fairly stiff paper to which the print is carefully glued with wallpaper paste or lightly taped. The whole thing is backed by protective cardboard (G).

edge at least 3 feet long. Since the metal has a tendency to slide out of position during cutting, glue some fine sandpaper along its underside. This will prevent the sliding. Place several old newspapers under the cardboard and cut firmly. The angle at which you hold the blade will determine the bevel of the cut, and whether it is straight or beveled is up to you. The knife should be sharp enough to cut easily with one smooth stroke. Pull the knife toward you as you cut. Keep a sharpening stone handy for frequent resharpening of the cutting edge.

After the mat is cut, position the print properly behind the hole and fasten it lightly to the back of the mat. It can then be adhered with gummed paper tape. Some printmakers place an extra sheet of blank print paper behind the print. The print is then protected with a backing of ordinary cardboard cemented with wallpaper paste or one of the casein glues produced specifically for use on paper.

The white surface of a mat dirties very easily. Most of the smudges and dirt can be removed with ordinary art gum erasers. Greasy finger marks will need rubbing with white powdered pumice, which can be purchased at many drug- or hardware stores. Use a clean cotton cloth to rub the pumice into the surface of the cardboard. If the prints are going into a sales and rental gallery or are going to be subjected to rough handling, it is a wise precaution to protect them with clear acetate. Some printers object to the reflections that this causes, but rough handling can destroy a print. The acetate should be as thin as possible. Stretch it tightly over the front of the matted print, fold it down, and fasten it to the back with gummed or masking tape. If the prints are going on an extensive exhibition circuit, such protection is mandatory. The hanging of the prints will be facilitated if you punch into each corner of the mat a white eyelet similar to the kind used in tennis shoes.

Framing serigraphs is primarily a matter of personal decision. Since serigraphs rarely have the weight of oil paintings, they are usually presented in simpler, smaller frames. Prints are mounted under a mat and generally framed under glass with the back and edges sealed against changes in humidity. Prints given a careful spraying of clear plastic can be framed without glass, but much more care must be taken with the mounting to prevent the print from buckling. Rubber cement should not be used in mounting prints. Wallpaper paste is preferred, as are the new casein glues especially prepared for paper. The cardboard used for mounting should be smooth and absorbent. First coat the back of the print with the glue so that the paper will expand before the print has adhered, then coat the mounting board. Allow both to set until they get tacky. Both glue coats should be very thin and set long enough to be absorbed into the surface. This will prevent the glue from oozing out beyond the edges. Place the print and mounting board together carefully, and cover the print with a piece of clean unprinted newsprint or white wrapping paper. Roll the print carefully with a

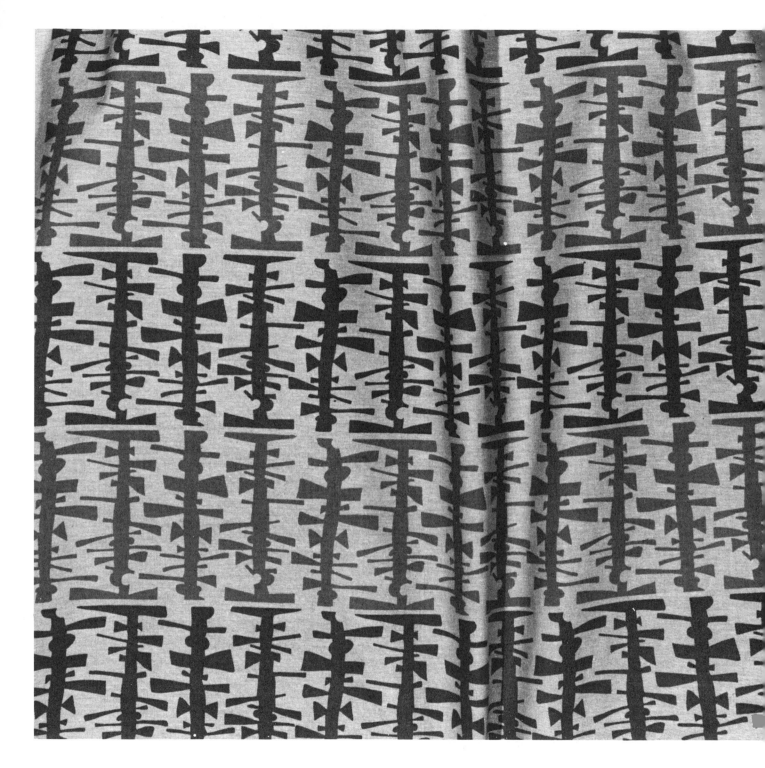

rubber roller, starting from the center of the print and working out toward the edges.

Fig. 9–4. The stencil for this two-color textile print was made with Profilm. ("Pines," by Sue Churchill Powell)

Display of Textiles

Printed textiles present far fewer problems than paper prints in mounting for display. Wall hangings are usually stiffened at the top with an inconspicuous bar of metal or wood. A cord fastened to each end of the bar allows the fabric to be hung. Occasionally the bottom of the textile may be weighted with a similar bar of wood or metal. Textiles are frequently designed to be hung on a wall and are not necessarily repeated patterns. Repeated patterns

131

can also be used as wall hangings with great success, although they are usually cut up and rearranged for clothing, pillows, or the like. These varied uses often determine the nature of a design, but this does not preclude textile designs printed for pure pleasure and self-expression.

Storing Your Work

Fabrics ready for printing and finished textiles can be successfully stored if rolled on tubes of cardboard or old newspaper. They remain free from creases and wrinkles and may be easily rolled out when needed. Thirty-six-inch rolls and other full widths can be placed upright in tall cartons in most household closets. Narrower widths can go on shelves or in drawers for convenient access. If the title of the design is written on protective wrapping paper around the roll, it can be identified more quickly.

Prints are safer stored in portfolios, which can be laid flat on shelves or in shallow (but wide and deep) drawers. Again, the title of the edition can be labeled on the outside of each portfolio. Having one portfolio that contains one or more copies of all your current work facilitates preparation for sales and exhibitions. Because of the relatively heavy layer of ink on a serigraph, the surface is subject to creasing, cracking, and scratching. Avoid touching the surface of a serigraph and do not fold or crease one. Even rolling a print should be avoided. If absolutely necessary, it should be rolled loosely (a minimum of 4 inches in diameter). Storing rolled prints is very hazardous since they are subject to creasing if any weight is placed on them inadvertently, and the paint may be loosened from the paper and flake off. Also, rolled prints are more difficult to mat and frame. Never pull a print out from the center of a stack. This is likely to result in a scratch or abrasion. Remove the top copies until you reach the one you wish.

Exhibition and Sale of Work

Both the serigrapher and the textile designer should consider the possible exhibition of their work. The exhibition is not usually a commercially profitable activity, but it is the necessary public testing of the artist's idea. Many exhibitions are juried, and whatever faults may be found with the jury system, it still represents the best outside test an artist can find for his work. But no single exhibition success or failure should be taken too seriously. The designer or serigrapher who participates in a fair number of competitive exhibitions will get a somewhat useful judgment of the quality of his work. Exhibitions range from the very large national and international ones with thousands of entries to the very small local ones. They vary a good deal. Art magazines usually list them well in advance and anyone wishing to compete can send

for an entry blank and information. It is a time-consuming and somewhat expensive endeavor. You must be prepared to face entry fees and transportation costs as well as packing expenses. Most exhibitions will pay for returning work that has been accepted, but usually the printer pays for transportation to the exhibition as well as the return costs if his work is rejected.

Those interested in selling their work will find it more useful to deal with private galleries and agents. Most will take work on consignment. When the artist is pricing his work, he should realize that anywhere from 30 to 40 per cent of the price is the commission paid to the gallery. Agents usually get as much as 50 to 75 per cent of the retail price, but remember that an agent can often sell an entire edition. When delivering work to a gallery or agent, the artist is usually expected to furnish a complete listing of the works, including the retail price (which includes the gallery's commission), in duplicate. The gallery will keep one copy and the artist the other. It is wise to get a signed contract that stipulates how long the work will be left at the gallery as well as the financial arrangements. The artist usually must agree not to sell a print for less than the gallery charges for the same print. Galleries often put considerable effort into promoting the artist and his work.

Serigraphs and textiles shipped to exhibitions should be carefully labeled and identified. For the textile designer, the roll is a convenient way to ship or transport pieces with a minimum of wrinkling. Serigraphs should be protected first with clean newsprint or tissue paper on each surface, then wrapped together in clean wrapping paper. Placing the prints face to face gives further protection. The package then is protected with a thin sheet of plywood on one side and corrugated cardboard on the other side. This in turn is wrapped in heavy wrapping paper. Constructing a wooden case for shipping is more expensive but a good investment if much use is anticipated.

The artist or designer does not have very adequate protection against the unwarranted display or reproduction of his work. And in most cases the court costs and procedures involved in fighting it are far too expensive. But if he is interested, he gets some protection if he does the following: somewhere on the print or fabric he should place a copyright symbol © and his signature. It can be incorporated in one of the color runs and printed. It is not necessary to register this copyright or pay any fees to have a valid binding copyright. However, if he wishes to start a suit, then he would have to register it, submit a copy of the work, and pay the registration fee. Additional protection is assured if he accompanies the sale of each work with a bill that has this statement printed on it: "All reproduction rights are reserved by the artist."

The problem for the textile designer is even greater. The pirating of a design can be easily accomplished if the pirate changes only some small part of the design, which, in theory, produces a new design.

GLOSSARY

Acetate—A clear or translucent plastic material upon which an image is painted in opaque paint to produce a resist with light-sensitive emulsion.

Acetic Acid—Used in a 5 per cent solution similar to household vinegar to neutralize the alkalinity of some screen-mesh cleaners and prepare the screen mesh for easy acceptance of emulsion-based resists.

Acetone—Solvent for hardened paint and lacquer; must be used with great care—away from fire—in a well-ventilated area.

Alcohol—Solvent for shellac.

Ammonium Bichromate—Chemical added to the gelatin emulsion to make the emulsion light sensitive. See **Potassium Bichromate**.

Anthrasol—Dyestuffs used in paste form for textile printing. Indigosol is another trade name for the same type of dyestuffs.

Art Deco—The style of decorative and applied design common in the early 1930s. The interior of Radio City Music Hall in New York City is an excellent example. It is characterized by a streamlined geometric line pattern.

Artist's Proof—A print produced during the development of an edition that is not included in the edition but that is of high enough quality for the artist to be willing to sign it.

Art Nouveau—The style of decorative and applied design common at the end of the nineteenth century. It is characterized by a writhing, curvilinear line and an asymmetrical form and is organic in feeling.

Backprinting—Ink picked up on the underside of the printing frame in textile printing. It is caused by printing over a wet print.

Benzene—Solvent for rubber cement; must be used only in a well-ventilated area.

Bleach (Household)—Solvent for photogelatin-emulsion resist (usually used in a 50 per cent solution with water). Will also remove some ink stains on the screen mesh. Must be used only on nylon or metal screen meshes.

Blockout—The material used in or on the screen mesh to form those parts of the stencil that are impervious to the printing medium. See **Resist**.

Bridging—In stencil forms the little bands of the stencil material left to prevent the floating parts (such as the center of the letter "O") from falling out of the stencil after it has been cut.

Bridging

Brush Printing—A method used in the textile industry before World War I. The color was applied with stiff brushes through a cardboard or zinc stencil. The spray gun soon replaced the brush.

Butyl Acetate—A solvent for lacquer. It will also remove hardened paint and paint stains from the screen mesh. Must be used only in a well-ventilated area.

Carbon Tetrachloride—Solvent for stains and paints on the screen mesh. Extremely toxic and should be used only in a well-ventilated area. Regulations govern its sale.

Casein Glue—A white glue that dries colorless. A thin or weak solution makes an adhesive for fastening a textile to the board while printing it. Also used in mounting a serigraph.

Caustic Soda—Sodium hydroxide, used in cleaning nylon screen mesh; sometimes called lye.

Cellulose-Based Printing Ink—A brilliant, somewhat expensive color used in printing.

Chalking a Design—Test-printing a design by powdering dry chalk through the stencil resist to space it and check the register on the printing board.

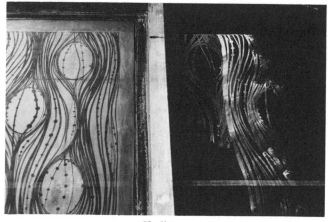

Chalking

Circle Cutter—A stencil-cutting knife that will produce a circle in a lacquer film stencil resist. It works like compasses.

Clear Base—See **Toner Base**.

Crystal Base—See **Toner Base**.

Derma Printing Method—A drawing is made on stencil with an ink containing an acid that eats into the paper to remove the areas to form a stencil for printing.

Direct Process of Fabric Printing—The color is printed directly on fabric through the open areas of the stencil resist.

Direct Method in Photogelatin Resist—Light-sensitive gelatin is applied directly on the screen mesh and exposed to light. See **Transfer Method; Double Transfer Method**.

Discharge Process of Fabric Printing—The fabric is dyed, and then a paste containing a bleaching agent is printed on it through the open areas in the stencil resist. The paste bleaches the pattern on the fabric.

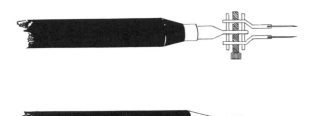

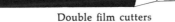

Double film cutters

Gauge stick: gauge bolts (*A*); gauge bar (*B*); distance between design units (*C*)

Double Film Cutter—A stencil knife that cuts a double line with two adjustable blades. It is used to produce lines of different widths on a lacquer-film stencil.

Double Transfer in Photogelatin Resist—The gelatin is sensitized on one base, transferred to a second base and exposed (often while wet), and when washed out transferred a second time to the screen mesh. When dry the base is removed and the printing resist is formed. See **Direct Method; Transfer Method.**

Dry Cleaner—Used to remove wax or paraffin and stains from the screen mesh.

Dry Copy-Printing Machine—A machine using heat to transfer or copy printed material.

Durometer—The rating method used in indicating the hardness of the rubber blade in the printing squeegee. Forty-five durometers is a soft and 80 durometers a very hard rubber blade.

Dye Paste—Viscous dyes including acid dyes, basic dyes, direct dyes, discharge dyes, fiber-reactive dyes, household dyes, prepared vat dyes, soluble vat dyes. Used by small-volume printers for textiles.

Edition of Prints—The number of finished, approved, and signed prints of the same design, produced by an artist.

Enamel—Available for screen-process printing in two types: (1) a fast-drying enamel that cannot be used outdoors without the protection of overprint varnish; (2) a high-gloss synthetic enamel that is very permanent and can often be baked onto the printing surface.

Enzyme Digester—A commercially prepared formula that removes gelatin-emulsion resists from the screen mesh after printing.

Extender—An additive for printing process paints that increases bulk and therefore reduces printing costs. Can be used up to one part extender to fifteen parts paint before the opacity and brilliance of the color are affected.

Fiber-Reactive Dye—Developed in 1956 by Imperial Chemical Industries, Limited, and produced under the trade name Procion. Used in textile printing for transparent and brilliant colors.

Film Line Cutter—See **Scooper Cutter.**

Film Presensitized Photo Emulsion—Commercially available photo emulsions on acetate bases, used to produce a photo resist.

Floating Part—The parts of a stencil that will fall away after the stencil is cut. For example, the center of the letter "O."

Fluorescent Paint—Available for printing—colors that "glow."

Free Lacquer Stencil—A "free" stencil resist formed by dripping, scraping, brushing, stippling, or dribbling lacquer over the surface of the screen. Creates attractive, textural prints for textile printing.

Gasoline—Solvent for asphaltum; must be used with great care—away from fires and in a well-ventilated area.

Gauge Bolt—A bolt fastened on the printing-board rail that fixes the distance between each printed design in the keying of a textile print.

Gauge Stick—Two gauge bolts placed on a stick (similar to a yardstick) to measure the exact distance needed to key the pattern. Used to set all the gauge bolts on the rail. Can also be filed to preserve the pattern key for future printing.

Gelatin—Ordinary household gelatin used in the light-sensitive photo-emulsion stencil resist.

Gelatin Emulsion—A light-sensitive mixture of gelatin, ammonium bichromate, Keltex, Calgon, and dye. Portions exposed to light become water insoluble.

Glycerin—Used with tempera poster paint in screen-process printing to retard the drying time.

Hide Glue—A brown heavy glue used in diluted form in a tusche-glue stencil. It is water soluble when dry.

Impasto—A heavy raised area produced by printing an extremely thick layer of ink. This can be achieved by using a thicker paper- or cardboard-stencil resist or by printing the same color area a number of times.

Indigosol—See **Anthrasol.**

Intaglio Printing—The image to be printed is scratched with a needle or etched with acid in the surface of the printing plate. This trough carries the ink.

J Bar—A hooked meter bar that secures the textile printing frame to the key rail to keep it firmly in place while printing.

Keltex—A commercial thickener used in the production of light-sensitive gelatin emulsion and in screen-printing dye pastes.

Kerosene—Solvent for wet enamel paint, lithographic crayon and tusche, oil- and varnish-based screen-process paints, oil-based texture paint, wax crayon.

Key Bolts—The adjustable bolts placed on the key rail to register a textile design in printing. Carpenter's stair gauges are frequently used. See **Gauge Bolt.**

Keying—The process of adjusting each printing frame so that successive colors are printed in exactly the right place.

Key Rail—The rail on one or both sides of the textile-printing board used to key the printing frame in repeating the design.

Kodalith Film—An orthochromatic high-contrast photographic film that can be exposed in a camera or with an enlarger to form a negative or positive. Can be used in producing a photo-emulsion resist.

Lacquer-Based Paint—A brilliant, fast-drying paint that can be used in printing a serigraph.

Lacquer-Film Resist—A thin coating of lacquer adhered to a heavy sheet of acetate or wax paper.

Lacquer-Film Solvent—Solvent for lacquer. Must be used only in a well-ventilated area.

Lacquer Thinner—A volatile liquid used to thin lacquer. Solvents for lacquer must be used only in a well-ventilated area.

Liquid Brush Cleaner—Will remove hardened paint from the screen mesh.

Maskoid—A rubber-based solution sometimes used for the original design in a wash or a stencil resist, with glue as the second material.

Mat—The cardboard placed over the print to separate it from its surroundings with a blank space. Makes the print more presentable.

Mat Knife—A strong, heavy, sharp knife (similar to a stencil knife with a single blade) used to cut the mat.

Mineral Spirits—Solvent for wet enamel paint, oil-based lacquer, lithographic crayon and tusche, oil- and varnish-based screen-process paints, oil-based textile paint, wax crayon.

Mitograph—A term given to the commercial product of screen-process printing by Albert Kosloff.

Mixing Varnish—A varnish material added to printing varnishes to improve their printing qualities.

Naphtha—Solvent for wax paraffin in the screen mesh. Should be used with care in a well-ventilated area.

Negative Space—In a design or composition the area between and around the main objects and forms. For example, the space behind and between the people in a group portrait. See **Positive Space.**

Positive (1) and negative space (2)

Negative Stencil—A stencil in which the resist material is the actual image and the background is printed.

Nufilm—An improved lacquer film for the production of a lacquer-film stencil, developed after Profilm.

Oleum—Solvent for wet enamel paint, lithographic crayon and tusche, oil- and varnish-based screen-process paints, oil-based textile paint, wax crayon.

Opacity—The quality of a thing that does not allow light to penetrate it. In printing, an opaque color will cover the color underneath and not be affected by it. See **Transparency.**

Overprinting—Printing one or more colors over each other, thus creating a new color and sometimes a new shape.

Overprint Varnish—A varnish printed over poster screen-process colors to make them permanent for outdoor use.

Paint Thinner—Solvent for wet enamel paint, lithographic crayon and tusche, oil- and varnish-based screen-process inks, oil-based textile ink, wax crayon.

Paper Stencil—A stencil resist cut from a sheet of paper.

Paper-Transfer Printing—The transfer of a design or photograph to a clear acetate with a dry copy-printing machine.

Photo-Emulsion Resist—A stencil resist composed principally of gelatin and a sensitizer that makes the gelatin water insoluble upon exposure to light. The unexposed portions are washed away with warm water creating the photo resist.

Pigment in Water Emulsion—A specialty ink that can be used to print textiles. Tends to have a slight stiffening effect on fabric.

Pinholes—Fine holes in a stencil resist.

Planographic Printing—The image is on the actual surface of the plate. The image is treated so that it holds the greasy ink while the wet surface of the rest of the plate repels the ink.

Pochoir—A method of stencil printing developed in France. Using a brush and water colors, the artist makes prints or copies of paintings with the aid of paper stencils. While originally used to copy other art, it has recently been used by some artists for original works.

Positive Space—In a design or composition the main objects and forms such as the people in a group portrait. See **Negative Space.**

Positive Stencil—The resist material fills the background of the design and the actual image is printed.

Potassium Bichromate—Chemical added to the gelatin emulsion to make the emulsion light-sensitive. Not as sensitive as ammonium bichromate. See **Ammonium Bichromate.**

Printing Board—The surface on which the paper or fabric is placed when printing. For textile printing it is padded.

Printing Frame—The frame, usually of wood, upon which the screen fabric is stretched.

Procion—A trade name for fiber-reactive dyes.

Profilm—A lacquer-type film adhered to wax paper. The lacquer is cut and peeled off to form a stencil resist.

Proof Prints—Trial or sample prints not identical to the rest of the prints in an edition, but whose quality is such that the artist is willing to sign them and label them as proof prints.

Pumice—A fine white powder used in cleaning a mat or screen.

Random Printing—The design unit is printed in several spots on a printing area without any predetermined placement. An irregular pattern develops.

Register Marks—Small crosses in the four corners of a design that help in placing the stencil on the screen precisely each time for multicolor printing.

Relief Printing—The image to be printed stands out in relief on the printing block, and this raised surface carries the ink.

Resist—Any stencil material that is adhered or applied to the silk or other fabric stretched on a printing frame. It holds back the printing medium, preventing its passage through the screen meshes. See **Blockout**.

Resist Process of Fabric Printing—A specially prepared paste is printed on the fabric through the open spaces in the stencil resist. The fabric is then dyed and the paste in the textile pattern resists the dye color.

Retarder—A liquid added to screen-process paint to slow up the drying time and help prevent screen clogging during the printing process. Especially valuable when humidity is low.

Roller Printing—A relief method for printing textiles in which the pattern or design is on a large inked drum or roller that makes contact with the textile to print the design. Commonly used by the textile printing industry.

Scooper Coater—A metal trough used to apply a gelatin emulsion to the screen fabric.

Scooper Cutter—A sharp knife for cutting fine lines in a lacquer-film stencil. The cutting edge is a small circle of steel sharpened on the inside of the circle. It scoops off the lacquer film. Also known as film line cutters or scratch tools.

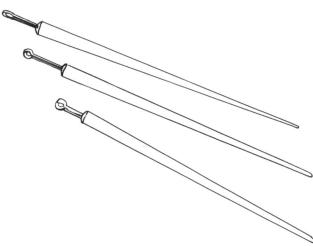

Scooper cutters, or film line cutters

Screen-Process Industry—The commercial industry that uses the screen process as a method of printing.

Selectasine—A screen printing process in which several colors are printed with one screen by successive blocking out of various areas of the screen.

Serigraph—A print made by the screen-process method for fine-art purposes.

Serigrapher—One who makes serigraphs.

Shibu—The varnish used by the Japanese to cover and protect their stencils and also to hold the fine hairs or silk threads that tie the floating parts to the main stencil in place.

Sizing—A material, usually starchlike, in most commercially printed cloth that adds "body." Sizing must be thoroughly washed out of the fabric before it can be safely printed.

Soap Flakes—Used to thicken tempera paint for screen-process printing. Makes tempera more acceptable in the printing frame.

Spray nozzle with adjustable pressure

Spray Pressure Nozzle—A commercial nozzle that can give both a fine spray and a power-jet stream of water for cleaning gelatin-emulsion stencils for printing and for cleaning the screen mesh after printing.

Squeegee—The rubber blade in a wooden holder, used to pull the printing medium from one side of the printing frame to the other over the stencil resist. A simple squeegee can be made of cardboard.

Steam Box—A metal box designed to heat-set dye printed on a textile without wetting any part of the textile.

Stencil—A material (paper, emulsion, film, etc.) from which certain areas have been removed. When the stencil is laid on a surface, color applied to it passes through the holes and prints on the surface below.

Swivel Stencil Cutter—A stencil knife that revolves freely making it easier to cut a curved line on a lacquer-film stencil.

T Plate—A metal "T" screwed at the center of each end of the textile printing frame and used in keying the frame.

Thinner—A liquid added to screen-process paint to increase its flow and its printing quality.

Toner Base—Sometimes called crystal base or clear base. A transparent syrupy solution that improves the printing quality of inks and helps to overcome the tendency of some screen colors to flake off when dry.

Transfer Method of Photogelatin Resist—Light-sensitive gelatin supported on a base, usually of acetate, is exposed to light. After the unexposed portion, which remains water soluble, is washed out, the exposed portion of gelatin, which has become water insoluble, and the acetate are transferred to the screen mesh by gentle pressure. When dry, the acetate base is peeled off, leaving the printing resist.

Transparency—The quality of allowing light to show through. A transparent color will not blot out and will be changed by the color underneath. See **Opacity**.

Transparent Base—A thick material (looks like Vaseline) used to extend the printing coverage of screen-process paints and increase their transparency. Usually made of aluminum stearate.

Transparent Toner Color—A highly concentrated color that is mixed with a crystal type of transparent base to produce a printing color.

Trisodium Phosphate—A wall cleaner available in most paint stores and used to clean the screen fabric. Removes grease from the screen mesh.

Turpentine—Solvent for wet enamel paint, lithographic crayon and tusche, oil- and varnish-based screen-process inks, oil-based textile ink, wax crayon.

Tusche—A thick black greasy liquid painted on the screen fabric in producing a glue-tusche stencil resist. Often called lithographic tusche, also available in crayon form.

Tusche-Glue Resist—A washout screen resist in which lithographic tusche is used to draw or paint the design on the screen fabric and then is coated with a glue solution. When the glue has dried the tusche is washed out with paint thinner or turpentine, producing the stencil desired.

Urea—A chemical used in the screen-printing paste for a fiber-reactive dye.

Wallpaper Paste—A starch-based paste used occasionally in mounting prints.

Washout Resist—A screen-stencil resist that is made by applying the design to the screen with one material and then covering the entire screen mesh with a second material; the first is then washed out with the proper solvent. See **Tusche-Glue Resist.**

Water-Based Textile Ink—An ink in a water base, which must be heat-set after being printed on a textile. Its stiffening effect on the textile is usually minimal.

Xylol—Solvent for rubber cement. Must be used with great care in a well-ventilated area only.

Yuzen Style—A Japanese method of making a stencil. Two identical stencils were cut, with the floating parts held in place by a cross grid of human hair or fine silk. The two stencils were varnished and placed together with the hair grid between the two stencil sheets.

BIBLIOGRAPHY

Ahlberg, G., and Jarneryd, O., *Block and Silk Screen Printing*. Sterling. 1961.

American Fabrics Magazine, editors of, *Encyclopedia of Textiles*. Prentice-Hall, 1960.

Anderson, Donald M., *Elements of Design*. Holt, Rinehart & Winston, 1961.

Auvil, Kenneth W., *Serigraphy: Silk Screen Techniques for the Artist*. Prentice-Hall, 1965.

Ballinger, Louise B., and Vroman, Thomas, *Design: Sources and Resources*. Reinhold, 1965.

Beitler, Ethel Jane, and Lockhart, Bill, *Design for You*. John Wiley, 1961.

Biegeleisen, J. I., *Complete Book of Silk Screen Printing Production*. Dover, 1963.

———, *The Silk Screen Printing Process*. McGraw-Hill, 1938.

———, *Silk Screen Stencil Craft as a Hobby*. Harper, 1935.

———, and Busenbark, E. J., *The Silk Screen Printing Process*. McGraw-Hill, 1941.

———, and Cohn, M. A., *Silk Screen Stencilling as a Fine Art*. McGraw-Hill, 1942.

———, and Cohn, M. A., *Silk Screen Techniques*. Dover, 1958.

Bindewald, Erwin, and Kasper, Karl. *Fairy Fancy on Fabrics*. Georg Westermann Verlag, Braunschweig, Germany, 1951.

Birrell, Verla, *The Textile Arts*. Harper, 1959.

Birren, Faber, *Creative Color*. Reinhold, 1961.

Brooks, Evelyn, *Your Textile Printing*. Charles A. Bennett, 1950.

Cahn, Joshua Binion, ed., *What is an Original Print?* Print Council of America, 1964.

Carr, Frances, *Guide to Screen Process Printing*. Pitman, 1962.

Chieffo, Clifford, *Silk Screen as a Fine Art*. Reinhold, 1967.

Clemence, Will, *The Beginner's Book of Screen Process Printing*. Blanford Press, London, 1959.

Conran, Terence, *Printed Textile Design*. Studio Publications, 1957.

Cronar Screen Process Film, E. I. Dupont De Nemours & Co. Photo Products Department, Wilmington, Delaware.

Dyeing and Printing with I. C. I. Dyestuffs. I. C. I. Organics, Inc., 1967.

Emerson, Sybil, *Design: A Creative Approach*. International Textbook, 1955.

Fossett, Robert O., *Techniques in Photography for the Silk Screen Printer*. Signs of the Times, 1959.

Giambruni, Helen, "Color Scale and Body Scale"; *Craft Horizons*, Vol. 28, No. 3, pp. 43–47, May/June 1969.

Green, Peter, *Creative Printmaking*. Batsford Publishing Company, London.

Heller, Jules, *Printmaking Today*. Holt, Rinehart & Winston, 1958.

Hiett, Harry L., *Screen Process Production*. Signs of the Times, 1936.

Jacobson, Egbert, *Basic Color*. Paul Theobald, 1948.

Johnston, Meda Parker, and Kaufman, Glen, *Design on Fabrics*. Reinhold, 1967.

Jones, Owen, *Grammar of Ornament*. B. Quartich, London, 1868.

Justema, William, *The Pleasures of Pattern*. Reinhold, 1969.

Kinsey, Anthony, *Introducing Screen Printing*. Watson-Guptill, 1968.

Kosloff, Albert, *Ceramic Screen Printing*. Signs of the Times, 1962.

———, *Elementary Silk Screen Printing*. Naz-Dar Co., 1951.

———, *Photographic Screen Process Printing*. Signs of the Times, 1962.

———, *Screen Printing Electronic Circuits*. Signs of the Times, 1968.

———, *Screen Process Printing*. Signs of the Times, 1964.

Lauterberg, Lotti, *Fabric Printing*. Reinhold, 1963.

Mansfield, Patricia Klein, *The Exploration of a Presensitized Screen Process Film for Designing Screen Printed Textiles*. Thesis, University of Wisconsin Memorial Library, 1966.

Marsh, Roger, *Silk Screen Printing for the Artist*. Transatlantic.

Nelson, George, *Problems of Design*. Whitney Publications, 1957.

Proud, Nora, *Textile Printing and Dyeing*. Reinhold, 1965.

Roberts, Edith A., "Silk Screen Printing with Anthrasol Indigosol Dyes." *Craft Horizons*, Vol. 18, p. 40, September/October 1958.

Robinette, G., *The Design Characteristics of Plant Materials*. Plant Form Studies, 1967.

Russ, Stephen, *Fabric Printing by Hand*. Watson-Guptill, 1968.

Searle, Valerie, and Clayson, Roberta, *Screen Printing on Fabric*. Watson-Guptill, 1968.

Shokler, Harry, *Artists Manual for Silk Screen Print Making*. Tudor Publishing Co., 1960.

Spurny, Jan, *Modern Textile Designer: Antonin Kybal*. Artia, Czechoslovakia, 1960.

Steffen, Bernard, *Silk Screen*. Pitman Publishing Co., 1963.

Stephenson, Jessie B., *From Old Stencils to Silk Screening: A Practical Guide*. Scribner, 1953.

Sternberg, Harry, *Silk Screen Color Printing*. McGraw-Hill, 1942.

Teur, Andrew W., *Japanese Stencil Designs* (book at Chicago Art Institute).

Zahn, Bert, *Silk Screen Methods of Reproduction*. Frederick J. Drake, 1950.

FILMSTRIP

"Screen Process Printing for the Serigrapher and Textile Designer,"
35mm color filmstrips (4 parts) which may be used in conjunction
with this book in the classroom, is available from—

International Film Bureau Inc.
332 So. Michigan Ave.   Chicago, Ill. 60604

INDEX